ENGAGED! ADVANCED PRAISE

"Gregg Lederman hits the bull's-eye in his new book, *ENGAGED!* He understands that inspired employees who live your organization's values have a lot more impact on your brand than fancy logos and slick advertising. If you want motivated people and raving fan customers, read this book!"

—Ken Blanchard, co-author of *Raving Fans* and *Trust Works!*

"Creating loyal employees and customers is a journey. A consistently great experience is required. *ENGAGED!* is a fantastic read for those looking for a step-by-step pathway to improve their employee and customer experience."

—Colleen Wegman, President, Wegmans Food Markets

"This is an excellent book that shows you how to build a high-performance company by creating and rewarding high-performance people."

—Brian Tracy, *New York Times* best-selling author of *Eat That Frog*

"Finally, a book that is so fundamental to success in today's business climate. Both managers of small businesses and multinationals can equally benefit from reading *ENGAGED!* Every leader or potential leader should read this. It's a fun and fresh reminder of how any brand can establish a culture with employees that your customers will love you for."

—Kyle O'Brien, Executive Vice President of Sales, Chobani, Inc.

"An experience is being delivered at every interaction with your customers. *ENGAGED!* provides a simple step-by-step approach to help every employee get 'on-stage' to perform your company's experience. An amazing read for anyone responsible for ensuring a world-class customer experience."

—Jamey Rootes, President, Houston Texans

"If you want to create an amazing culture, one where employees are engaged, excited to come to work, desire to do their best, feel fulfilled, and want to make customers happy, then you will love the lessons you will learn in *ENGAGED!*"

—Shep Hyken, *New York Times* best-selling author of
The Amazement Revolution

"When leaders begin to care more about the company than they do for themselves, great things start to happen. If you are looking for a book packed with tools to help create winning teams, you just found it. An amazing read for anyone looking to enhance their leadership skills at work and in life."

—Mark Schlereth, three-time Super Bowl champion and
current ESPN NFL Analyst

"If you're looking to completely transform your customer experience, *ENGAGED!* provides the strategies, tools, and techniques to show you how."

—Lynn Yanyo, Director of Marketing and Customer
Services, LORD Corporation

"What a great book! It is practical, smart, has fresh energy, and is edgy. I really like the way Gregg Lederman puts theory into practice. Outstanding!"

—Craig P. Dinsell, EVP, Chief Human Resource Officer,
Oppenheimer Funds

"A fundamental principle of business first developed at and now widely touted by the Simon School is that 'skin in the game' matters. When individuals are more invested and engaged, the performance of their company improves. Gregg Lederman's book provides a novel method to quantify employee engagement and thereby ultimately a vehicle to improve your company's performance. For leaders who care about making their companies ever better, *ENGAGED!* is a must—first to read and then to put its insights into practice."

—Mark Zupan, Dean of the Simon School at the
University of Rochester

"Gregg Lederman in his book *ENGAGED!* has provided a common-sense approach to a not-so-common, yet critical, business strategy—that is, spending less time creating and marketing your brand and more time getting all employees to 'live the brand.' Approaches such as 'making the invisible visible' and creating a unified organizational 'mindset' are key concepts for leaders to ponder. Gregg makes the point that what is commonly defined by business strategists as the 'soft stuff' truly is the 'hard stuff' as evidenced by the absence of high levels of employee engagement in so many companies today. Want a straightforward approach to engaging more employees in the work of your organization? Open this quick-read book and begin to change your mindset!"

—Kathy Parrinello, Chief Operating Officer,
Strong Memorial Hospital, University of
Rochester Medical Center

"*ENGAGED!* is packed with tools and techniques to inspire any manager or executive. The strategic approach to employee recognition you will learn in this book has helped us to shape and sustain our 'best place to work' culture."

—Casey M. McGuane, Chief Operating Officer,
Higher One (NYSE: ONE)

ENGAGED!

**Outbehave
Your Competition
to Create
Customers for Life**

ENGAGED!

*Outbehave
Your Competition
to Create
Customers for Life*

GREGG LEDERMAN
Author of *Achieve Brand Integrity*

ENGAGED!: Outbehave Your Competition to Create Customers for Life

Published by Evolve Publishing, Inc.
www.evolvepublishing.com

Cover and interior design by Ramsdell Design
Art design by Sherry Hardiman
Author photo by Walter Colley

978-0-9893222-1-8 paperback
978-0-9893222-2-5 ePUB
978-0-9893222-3-2 ePDF

Printed in the United States of America

10 9 8 7 6 5 4 3 2 1

Contents

Acknowledgments

It took a small army to bring *ENGAGED!* from concept to reality. Every employee on the Brand Integrity team provided input, as did many of the clients who we've worked with to create workforces filled with motivated and committed employees focused on creating customers for life. I owe many thanks to those who have shared their wisdom and experiences.

To my wife Karyn: Thank you for your support, especially during the intense weekend mornings packed with writer's block and content breakthroughs. Thank you for your patience as I went into overdrive for more than a year, obsessing about the importance of this book and the path that lay ahead.

To my daughters Caroline, Katie, and Lucy: You've helped me on this journey more than you could ever know. Your passion and energy for life is nearly impossible to keep up with. My desire to not give up our fun-filled weekends motivated my early morning, high-octane-caffeine-fueled writing sessions.

To the team at Brand Integrity: Through your work in developing our Experience Management software and continued refinement of the Achieving Brand Integrity process, you brought the strategic direction and content of *ENGAGED!* to life. I simply packaged it up in a book for the rest of the world to learn from. We really do keep our clients for life and you are the reason why.

To Courtney: There is only one person who can truly bring my voice to life and make it grammatically correct and fun to read. You've challenged assumptions, enhanced my prose, and been there every step of the way from initial manuscript to the pages ahead. And . . . you were nice enough to laugh at my jokes, too.

What to Expect from Your Journey Through *ENGAGED!*

Imagine . . . your entire workforce shares a common mindset—a way of thinking. This mindset is driven by deeply held values and beliefs that everyone in your company holds to be true. It's because of this mindset that people in your company tend to act a certain way. They interact with each other and customers in ways that lead to an experience—a truly *branded* experience your company has become known for.

Imagine everyone in your company is aligned and ENGAGED around the behaviors that are necessary to make that experience come to life. These behaviors are clearly documented, they're considered nonnegotiable, and they're performed consistently by employees in ways that lead to happy customers who are more than just loyal. Your customers are delighted, they *love* doing business with your company, and they are ENGAGED!

Your workforce is outbehaving the competition. They simply "behave" better than your competitors'.

This is not by chance. It is by design.

Imagine that your company has taken the powerful mindset (and nonnegotiable behaviors) and fully integrated them into the processes and systems for hiring new employees, ensuring they are truly indoctrinated into your company's way of thinking—its way of being.

Imagine these same behaviors are incorporated into job profiles to set clear and achievable expectations.

Imagine every employee performance review is not only based on the technical skills and tasks but also on the natural tendencies and abilities to perform the very experience your customers want most.

Imagine employee recognition is pervasive throughout your company. A daily dose of capturing and sharing examples of the mindset and nonnegotiable behaviors in action helps fuel the replication of the branded experience. Your branded experience is visible every day. Employees love to deliver it. Customers love to receive it.

Imagine customers have contributed to making you great by sharing their perspective on the experience of doing business with your company. Their feedback not only helps you improve, it is also regularly shared with the workforce to help them see the terrific impact they have on customers' lives.

Last, imagine every manager in your company truly understands that it's their job to manage the experience. Every manager is trained on the essential habits that make them more trusted leaders because they remind others about the importance of performing the behaviors and delivering your company experience. Your managers are expert at making the experience part of the conversation at work every day. They make decisions using your company mindset. They hold difficult, yet necessary, conversations and use the experience as their guide. And they are constantly capturing and sharing examples of the experience in action to help others learn, become inspired by, and replicate over and over again.

Your workforce is . . . highly ENGAGED. You know it because you've gone beyond simply announcing who you are and what you want to be known for. You haven't just told people what your culture is and tried to get them to do it. Rather, you've inspired them to search deep into who they are and why they should want to live your company's brand every day!

Every company, no matter what the industry or economic environment, can ENGAGE its workforce to deliver a consistently great customer experience. An experience that will in turn ENGAGE customers, leading to increased sales and profits. Every company can do this when it Manages the Experience.

For over a decade, my firm, Brand Integrity, has worked with companies who want to inspire an ENGAGED workforce to live their company's brand. At the time of this writing, over 60 percent of Brand Integrity's clients were noted on "best place to work" lists either in their region, industry, or on *FORTUNE's* 100 Best Companies to Work For annual ranking. In almost all cases, our clients are wildly profitable and continue to grow and prosper. These companies embrace and take action on the Eight Principles of success presented in this book.

In my last book, *Achieve Brand Integrity: Ten Truths You Must Know to Enhance Employee Performance and Increase Company Profits*, I introduced the concept of Brand Integrity as a business result. It's the end state you achieve when your company is known as who and what you say you are while reaching business goals—when all of your marketing messages and sales-speak are backed up and delivered upon.

It seems crazy to me that so many companies still create organizational silos between the employee view of the brand and the customer view of the brand. It's not only crazy, it's way too complicated. The brand is your image based on the experiences had by human beings. It is based on how you are BEING to human BEINGS! There is no need for separation of branding disciplines. This separation is a result of poorly designed silos in the workforce between sales, marketing, HR, and operations. To achieve Brand Integrity, all of these disciplines need to come together, and the company's managers need to recognize that there is really only one brand for the company based on an experience delivered. And that experience must be managed if a company is going to achieve an ENGAGED status with employees and customers.

Achieve Brand Integrity was delivered in a conversational style and tone, packed with energy, humor, and knowledge. You can expect that same combination from this book. What is different about *ENGAGED!* is the intense focus I will share on how to measure the experience, creating unheard of visibility among leaders in your company. These measures are not new in concept, only in application. You will learn proven methodologies that use readily available technology to quantify your culture and customer experience, helping you to make important business decisions to improve your work culture and customer loyalty. This is not simply another book on employee engagement (clearly not needed) or the customer experience (although many more are needed). The best practices shared in this book will enable you to measure whether employees are Living the Brand,[1] whether managers are Managing the Experience (being courageous, data-driven leaders), and whether customers are having the experience they want (do they love you? or at least like you a lot?).

From my experience, ENGAGED is what every company wants more of. With the time you invest in reading this book you will learn the Eight Principles that will help you get more ENGAGED employees and customers.

What do I mean by ENGAGED?

An ENGAGED workforce is made up of employees who are committed and motivated to act in the best interest of your company. ENGAGED customers fall in love with your company, are more loyal, proactively tell others about you, and buy more of your company's products and services (and do so more often). As you will learn, the benefits of engaging your workforce and customers are easy to see and difficult to refute.

Your journey is broken into two parts.

In Part 1 you will discover how to create a Living the Brand System[2] rooted in managerial and employee behavior. I will cover the topics of employee engagement and its impact on the customer experience as well as proven approaches for defining a mindset and experience that can be profitably delivered.

All businesses operate with systems. No business could work efficiently and effectively without them. You have HR

---

1. Living the Brand: when your employees KNOW the brand and DO it consistently by making it a part of their everyday lives at work.

2. Living the Brand System: an approach for defining, reminding others about, and quantifying the experience employees and customers have.

systems, distribution systems, customer service systems, financial systems, sales systems, etc. Just think of your company's C-suite. They're all managers in charge of critical systems.

LIVING THE BRAND SYSTEM

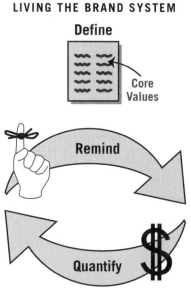

There is one system that works across all the systems in your company—a Living the Brand System. No one person or job function owns it. Pigeonholing it in HR can be detrimental because you end up with a bunch of fluffy values integrated into performance systems with poor expectation-setting and limited accountability. If you confine it to marketing, it can be harmful because then you're left with a bunch of promises that your employees are not empowered or motivated to keep.

A company must do three things to implement a Living the Brand System:

1. Clearly DEFINE the branded experience.[3] (Okay, I realize we're already on our third footnote. There are only a few in the whole book. It's important that you understand these key terms up front.)

---

3. Branded experience: an experience designed for employees and customers based on a common mindset and proprietary behaviors that are clearly documented, trained, measured, and reinforced.

2. REMIND employees about the delivery of the experience—clearly setting expectations, communicating, and holding everyone accountable.

3. QUANTIFY the experience and link it to financial results.

Defining the branded experience is the "simple" step. Engaging management with the reality that continuous reminding and quantifying is not only a management skill but also one that will make them much more trusted as leaders is considerably more difficult. In this book you will learn logical business theories that have been transformed into management tools, techniques, and measures that make it incredibly practical for defining, reminding employees about, and quantifying the branded experience.

While I am on the topic of reminding, let me share a little secret that I will refer back to throughout your journey through *ENGAGED!* When it comes to implementing an employee- and customer-focused branded experience, your success as a company (and as a manager) will be determined 1 percent or less on the training provided to the workforce and 99 percent or more by the ability of management to remind them. More to come on this little secret in the pages ahead—in fact, in Principle 8, you will see how your company can easily reach 150 reminders per manager a year.

SECRET TO SUCCESS

1% Training

99% **Reminding**

Part 2 will explore the necessary courage and data required to quantify the branded experience and hold it accountable (yes, you can and should hold the experience accountable) for delivering upon the financial results you already measure. You will be introduced to an approach for looking at your branded experience from a 360° View that includes employee, customer, and financial metrics. You will learn proven methodologies for learning from employees whether they are Living the Brand and gaining insights from customers as to whether they are witnessing the brand in action, leading them to refer your company and buy more of your products and services.

Each chapter will begin with a few highlights for those of you who are "skimmers." That way you can quickly determine how deep a dive you need to take with each of the Eight Principles. At the end of each chapter is a Power of the Pause section. The purpose of this section is to get you to slow down, linger for a moment, and think before moving on. Doing so will help you reflect on what you just learned and how you can apply it for maximum benefit in your company.

This is not a one-size-fits-all solution for defining, managing, and measuring your branded experience. My goal is to provide you with the right questions, methods, and metrics to evaluate and understand your current culture and customer experience to help you better understand the employee and customer perspective. The questions and insights I throw your way will lead you to answers best suited for YOUR business, for YOUR people, and for YOUR customers. Use this book to make the choice as to whether your company has what it takes to ENGAGE employees and ENGAGE customers.

When I refer to employees in a company, I mean all employees, including managers and senior leaders. Anyone who collects a paycheck is an employee. This is important because in no way do I want any readers to think that some portion of this material does not apply to them. When I refer to leaders or managers, I mean anyone who has the responsibility to lead employees. I will use the terms *leaders* and *managers* interchangeably throughout. If you are someone who has people who report to you, you're a supervisor or a manager and the learning from this book will be directly applicable. If you're not, but aspire to be one, the Eight Principles will help you with your career advancement.

HOW WOULD YOU RATE YOUR CULTURE TODAY?

Take a moment and rate how much you agree with the following statement.

Employees throughout our company are aligned, committed, and motivated (ENGAGED!) to deliver a consistently great customer experience.

Strongly Disagree				Neutral					Strongly Agree	
0	1	2	3	4	5	6	7	8	9	10
◯	◯	◯	◯	◯	◯	◯	◯	◯	◯	◯

Unless you scored a nine or ten, do not plan on simply skimming this book. Read the chapter highlights, but dive deep and explore the possibilities the Eight Principles present. Getting employees aligned, ENGAGED, and motivated is what it takes to deliver a branded experience that drives profitability. The following prose will show you how!

THE EXPERIENCE IS YOUR BRAND

A 2013 study found that 49 percent of executives believe customers will switch brands due to a poor customer experience. Even more interesting is that the same report found that 89 percent of customers say they have switched because of a poor customer experience. Do you think this trend will continue? I sure do. Because while the great majority of companies want to be good at delivering the customer experience, very few are investing the necessary resources to create the systems to define the experience and ensure it is consistently brought to life. As consumers we are fed up with tolerating employees in companies who act as if they are doing us a favor by providing . . . well . . . customer service. The latest research shows there are three main drivers of a bad customer experience, which are easily avoided with an ENGAGED workforce. The three drivers and how often they happen are:

1. Employee was rude: 73 percent
2. Employee was too slow to resolve my issue: 55 percent
3. Employee lacked the necessary knowledge: 51 percent

The experience is what employees and customers use to determine if they will be loyal to your company. Employees evaluate their work environment (the culture) and what it is like to work in your company, and that perception has a profound impact on their attitudes and actions. Customers evaluate their experience at every point of interaction with your company's people, products, and services. The experience impacts their willingness to continue purchasing. In both cases, the experience drives the brand image your company becomes known for. The experience creates engagement for both employees and customers.

In *Achieve Brand Integrity*, I outlined the Four Realities of Branding. I will share them again here to emphasize the point that the type of branding I am talking about has nothing to do with marketing the brand and everything to do with inspiring employees to *live* it.

The Four Realities of Branding

1 **Branding is not a part of the business, it is the business.** Every interaction an employee has with a coworker or a customer has the power to strengthen or hinder the brand image of your company.

2 **Branding is about experiences, not logos and taglines.** When was the last time you bought a product or service and continued to do so because you just loved the company logo? Enough said!

3 **The little things that you do CONSISTENTLY are much more important than the BIG things you say.** Ninety percent of the time we judge companies and determine whether we are going to do business with them based on the experience we have or someone we trust tells us about. Ten percent of the time or less our purchase decision is based on what the company tells us about how great it is.

4 **A Living the Brand strategy is the single most important differentiator between a good company and great company.** To deliver a consistently great experience, you need to have a system in place that helps integrate the branded experience into recruitment, selection, evaluation, and recognition of talent (a Living the Brand System).

LIVE THE BRAND!

ENGAGED employees Live the Brand to help their company achieve Brand Integrity. To Live the Brand means you KNOW the mission, values, brand positioning, guiding principles, etc., that your company has announced to the workforce and marketplace and you know how to DO them in your day-to-day job.

Before you dive into Principle 1: *Get Every Employee on Stage, Delivering the Experience for Customers*, pause and answer the following questions:

- Am I Living the Brand at work?
- Are employees around me consistently Living the Brand at work?
- Are customers ENGAGED because they consistently have the experiences they want?

The companies that consumers love to do business with have cracked the code on creating an ENGAGED workforce that Lives the Brand—they outbehave the competition. These companies get recognized as best places to work and get rewarded with ENGAGED customers who are incredibly loyal. These companies know the brand is about doing, not saying. You will read about best practices these companies use for making the brand a part of the hiring, performance evaluation, and recognition systems, as well as how they gather and share customer feedback. You will learn how they create measurable behaviors and objectively and passionately assess their ability to do them. You will learn how they create experiences that earn their customers' admiration and dare I say . . . love.

I invite you to join me, my teammates at Brand Integrity, and our clients on the journey to creating more ENGAGED customers with an ENGAGED workforce.

Please read on . . .

PART 1
Define a Living the Brand System

Get Every Employee on Stage, Delivering the Experience for Customers

---

HIGHLIGHTS

1. Your company delivers tons of experiences every day. Employees interact with each other and with customers, creating your company's branded experience. Therefore, the question is not are you delivering an experience? Rather, it's are you effectively Managing the Experience being delivered to ensure it is one that is consistent and profitable?

2. Every company wants an ENGAGED workforce that outbehaves the competition, making them "different" in a positive way—a way that customers will love them for. It is management's responsibility to make sure the experience is delivered, performed, and evaluated.

3. Every company shares the same purpose: to create and keep more profitable and ENGAGED customers. To achieve the purpose, you must have ENGAGED employees performing an experience that ENGAGES customers.

ONE COMPANY YOU LOVE

Allow me to take you on the journey of love. On this journey you will discover what causes someone to love to do business with a company and the benefits derived from such love.

To take this journey you will need to close your eyes and take a few deep breaths. I realize this may be a bit uncomfortable as we've only just met. You're going to have to trust me a few times throughout this book. This is one of them.

> "Ninety percent of the time people judge a company based on the experience they or someone else has and 10 percent or less based on the sales or marketing message."

When you have your eyes closed, I want you to think about a company that you love to do business with. You love to do business with this company because their people Live the Brand every day. It is clear to you, based on experience, that this company's employees understand who their company is and what the branded experience is all about.

Employees in this company not only KNOW the branded experience, they DO it consistently. This company is outbehaving their competition. Outbehaving the competition leads to incredible customer loyalty. Customers buy more and more often. Customers are less price-sensitive. You are less price-sensitive.

Employees in this company also seem to be quite ENGAGED. They recognize their employer as a great place to work. They are productive and happy.

This company is managing an experience for you. You love to do business with it so much that you've rewarded it with the ultimate compliment—your referral. You've shared your experience with others and suggest they try this company. Or maybe you simply tell others about this company because it feels good to do so. In essence, you've become an unpaid marketing department helping the company to get customers.

So take ten seconds and close your eyes. Think and reflect on a company you love because it is all the things I've just described. Think about a few companies. I'll wait . . .

After you're done reflecting, make a list of a few of the companies you love to do business with and note why. What do they do that makes you feel as though they've taken the time to understand the experience you desire? What is it that they do to deliver that experience for you? Make note of one or two things they do, big or small.

Companies I Love:	What They Do to Earn My Love:
_____	_____
_____	_____
_____	_____
_____	_____
_____	_____

One of the simple truths you will see throughout this book is, "It may be common sense, but that doesn't mean it is common practice." I'll bet your list has some specific actions (behaviors) ENGAGED employees do that help you to stay in love with the company they work for. These companies have mastered turning common sense into common practice. That is why you love to do business with them.

Leaders in the companies you love to do business with understand that KNOWING the brand and DOING the brand leads to stronger work cultures and more profitable customer relationships.

Employees in these companies you love recognize they are on stage orchestrating an experience. They appreciate that they have the ultimate responsibility and opportunity to deliver an experience—to perform an experience that makes customers happy. And in most cases, it makes them happy too.

"ALL THE WORLD'S A STAGE"

William Shakespeare coined the phrase, "All the world's a stage and all the men and women merely players." His quote is often taken out of context and has been debated among those much smarter than me with respect to poetry and the arts. That said, let me provide my interpretation of what Shakespeare really meant. At work, all employees (everyone who gets paid for doing a job at the company) are on stage responsible for delivering a branded experience to coworkers and customers.

That means that no matter how far removed your role is from the actual customer, you are still responsible for delivering an experience that helps those who do interact with the customer. *All* employees are on stage! Think about it. You are in the spotlight from the moment you enter your workplace in the morning until the moment you leave. Your coworkers and customers are watching what you do. They are watch-

"ALL THE WORLD'S A STAGE"

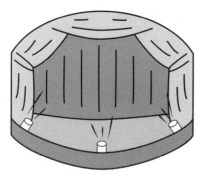

ing what you do more than they are listening to what you say. If you are a parent, you know that you are on stage with your kids in the same way. What do they pay more attention to: what you do, or what you say? If you tell them not to eat

6

candy, but they see you eating candy, which will they remember more?

OUTBEHAVE TO OUTPERFORM

Here is an example of an experience that does not help customers to fall in love. This story is a perfect example of how to market your brand and hope employees will deliver it.

I was checking into a hotel and was greeted by the front desk receptionist. She was wearing a button that said, SERVICE "10." This caught my attention so I immediately asked what level 10 service was all about. Unfortunately for the receptionist, here's how our conversation went:

ME: What is SERVICE "10"?

RECEPTIONIST: [BLANK STARE]

ME: Certainly it must mean something?

RECEPTIONIST: [LOOKING OVER TO THE MANAGER AT THE NEXT TERMINAL] What is 10 Service? Can you help me explain it?

I was thinking, "Never mind," but listened as the manager stumbled through an explanation.

Now, this was not a random motel on the interstate. It was a high-end hotel chain that any manager or leader would know about—one that sells rooms for more than $150 per night. I frequent this chain many times throughout the year. Later that day, inside the lobby, I found a sign telling customers that SERVICE "10" was the company's goal to provide great customer service. Considering that the main point of contact for checking in a guest didn't even know the definition of great service, I knew that my stay probably wouldn't deliver an experience worthy of rave reviews.

This is a perfect example of promoting an experience and failing to deliver it, which is why such companies cannot consistently "win." Winning companies understand that employees are constantly on stage, DOING the branded experience as part of their performance and orchestrating the memorable experiences that make us, as consumers, love them and refer them.

Now here is an example from Enterprise Rent-A-Car whose employees truly understand that they are on stage creating experiences customers will love. Their employees are ENGAGED, and the experience ENGAGES customers.

Let me set the stage (pun intended).

PRINCIPLE PLAYERS

GREGG (ME), *traveler, customer*

TERRY, shuttle driver

NICOLE, greeter

ASHLEY, service attendant

SUSAN, gate attendant

STEPHEN, service attendant

PATRICK, shuttle attendant

SCENE: Detroit Metro Airport on a particularly cold December morning

[1.1] GREGG waits on the curb—stressed and very late. Delta canceled the flight the night before, and he was rebooked on a 6 a.m. flight. He is scheduled to speak to an audience of senior executives

at 9 a.m. It's 8:15, and the drive to the event is about forty minutes. He has multiple speaking engagements in the area over the next few days, so grabbing a cab is not an ideal option.

[The Enterprise van approaches and the driver steps out.]

TERRY (ENGAGED EMPLOYEE): Hi folks, welcome to Detroit. We are glad you are here. My name is Terry and I will take you to get your car. Does anyone need any help with his or her bags?

[GREGG takes his seat along with several other passengers.]

TERRY: We appreciate your renting from Enterprise. I will have you safely to the rental car facility in about four minutes. When you get there you will find fresh coffee and snacks waiting for you.

[1.2] The van arrives at the Enterprise facility and the customers file out and collect their things. NICOLE stands in the entranceway, greeting customers as they arrive. GREGG approaches.

NICOLE (ANOTHER ENGAGED EMPLOYEE): Hi, I'm Nicole, welcome to Enterprise. What is your name?

GREGG: Gregg. Good morning, Nicole.

NICOLE: Welcome Gregg, step right up to the counter. Ashley's ready to help you get your car.

ASHLEY (ENGAGED!): Welcome, Gregg.

GREGG: Hi Ashley. I am very late this morning. My flight last night was canceled, and I had to fly out early this morning. I need to be on stage in forty-five minutes, and the venue is about forty minutes away. Anything you can do to help me get out of here faster would be greatly appreciated.

ASHLEY (SYMPATHETICALLY): *I will see what I can do!*

[Less than a minute later, ASHLEY leads GREGG out to his car.]

9

ASHLEY: Let me help you with that bag. Please get in and get yourself comfortable in the car. Here's a fresh bottle of water. I will look around the vehicle to make sure there is no unreported damage.

[Due to the friendliness and good service provided by TERRY, NICOLE, and ASHLEY so far, GREGG's trust in Enterprise is so great that he doesn't think twice about giving the car the once-over. He's confident ASHLEY is going to take care of it and act in his best interest.]

[1.3] ASHLEY finishes the walk around and sends GREGG on his way out. At the exit he meets the gate attendant, SUSAN, and hands her his paperwork.

SUSAN (ENGAGED EMPLOYEE): Hi, I'm Susan. How was our customer service?

GREGG: It was great. *(He is pleasantly surprised at the consistency of ENGAGED employees.)*

SUSAN: [handing the paperwork back] Terrific! Thank you for renting from Enterprise. Have a great day.

GREGG: Susan, what if I was to tell you that your customer service was not good?

SUSAN: Well, I would have asked you what happened and if it was not something I could have resolved for you I would have connected you to one of my managers who would make it right.

[Exit]

[1.4] Two days later. GREGG returns to the Enterprise center to drop off the car. There he is greeted by a service attendant, STEPHEN.

STEPHEN: Welcome back! My name is Stephen. I want to make sure we get you on the right van and back to the airport as quickly as possible. Which airline are you flying today?

GREGG: Delta.

STEPHEN: Okay, that van is about to leave. I'll signal to them to wait a moment for you. Don't forget your cell phone, keys, wallet, or any other important items.

[GREGG picks up his things and approaches the van.]

PATRICK: Hi, I'm Patrick. I'll be taking you safely back to the airport. *(Enthusiastically)* May I get that bag for you?

[GREGG and the other customers climb into the van.]

PATRICK: We appreciate all of you renting from Enterprise. I will have you back at the airport in about four minutes. Everyone ready? Well then, let's go!

[Exit]

Unlike the hotel employees from my first example, Enterprise employees recognize that they are performing in front of customers. They orchestrate an ideal experience at each interactive touchpoint by playing the role of "host." This experience is driven by a Living the Brand System—an approach for defining, reminding others about, and quantifying the branded experience employees can orchestrate at critical points of interaction. Experiences that create customer love.

If the hotel employees understood the important roles they play in delivering customer service, perhaps the SERVICE "10" flop would have been easier to

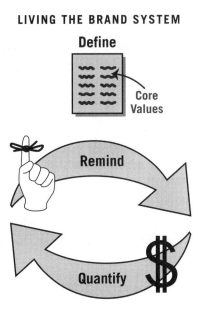

LIVING THE BRAND SYSTEM

Define

Core Values

Remind

Quantify

11

look past. However, in the same stay, employees blamed me for having the wrong check-out date in their computer system, billed me the wrong amount two out of the three nights I stayed there, and failed to deliver the complimentary *USA Today* each morning. (Other guests received their copies, so why didn't they treat me as a valuable member of their audience? Probably because I was too curious as to what SERVICE "10" was all about.)

As unpleasant as my hotel stay was, it emphasized the simple fact I've been making so far: On a week-to-week, day-to-day, hour-to-hour basis, your company's brand is being performed by employees who are delivering an experience for customers. On any given day they are either helping your company to outperform or underperform. Provide employees with the right mindset and help them understand the branded experience to be delivered and they will outbehave your competition, enabling your company to outperform the competition.

GET EVERYONE FOCUSED ON YOUR COMPANY'S PURPOSE

During keynote presentations and workshops, I frequently ask the audience, "What is the purpose of your company?" I drop a hint that every company has the exact same purpose. Inevitably, the majority of responses are that the purpose of a company is to make a profit. While this view may seem obvious, it fails to take into consideration what companies need to get there. So then I share wisdom from Peter Drucker, Harvard Business professor and management guru, who published a paper in 1986 stating that the purpose of every company is to create a customer. The audience typically reflects for a moment and then overwhelmingly agrees that while profit is the fundamental objective for every company, companies can't achieve it without creating and keeping customers. I've modified Drucker's quote a bit to better tie it to the end game business leaders are all striving for:

The purpose of a company is to create and keep *profitable* and *ENGAGED* customers!

A challenge many companies face is that they spend so much time trying to get new customers that they lose focus on the tremendous efficiencies that can be created by delivering a better experience to existing customers. This encourages them to buy more and even tell others to buy from them.

CUSTOMERS WHO LOVE YOU WILL SPEND MORE

According to research by Harris Interactive, consumers not only want a better experience but they will pay more for it. Even in a negative economy, 60 percent of consumers say a better experience is a high priority and one that they are willing to pay more for (either most of the time or always). On the flip side, another study found that 91 percent of unhappy customers will not willingly do business with your company again.

There has never been a better time to ENGAGE employees with the delivery of a well-orchestrated customer experience. Now is the time to outbehave. Now is the time to make sure you have a Living the Brand System in place. Customers want to love you. You are on stage. Start performing!

POWER OF THE PAUSE

- Do employees come to work knowing they are on stage, responsible for performing an experience for each other and for customers?
- Do managers in your company realize they have the ultimate responsibility to evaluate the performance of your branded experience?

Make Happy Employees to Create ENGAGED Customers

HIGHLIGHTS

1. Most companies have a vast reserve of untapped employee performance potential, where managers struggle to build emotional connections between employees and the company's success. The evidence is irrefutable—most workforces are filled with disengaged workers who are not willing to put in the extra discretionary effort that owners and managers want. The research tells us that 70 percent of workers are "not engaged" or are "actively disengaged" in their work, meaning they are emotionally disconnected from their workplace and are less likely to be productive. That leaves nearly one-third of workers who are "engaged," or involved in and enthusiastic about their work and contributing to their companies in a positive manner.

2. Lack of an ENGAGED workforce is a debilitating disease! If you had a debilitating disease in your body wouldn't you take care of it, right away? The definition of *debilitating* is something that interferes with the activity of daily living. Doesn't a disengaged employee interfere with the activity of daily work?

AN UNHAPPY EMPLOYEE CAN'T CREATE AN ENGAGED CUSTOMER

I kick-started my day in sunny Rochester, New York, just like any other Friday. I poured myself some coffee and sat down at the kitchen island with my morning paper (yes, I am one of the few who still subscribes to and reads the paper). The headline read "Wegmans [headquartered in Rochester] Ranks No. 4 on List of Best Places to Work." I thought to myself, "Well, it's that time of year again." Wegmans was once again ranked on the 100 Best Companies to Work For list compiled by *FORTUNE* and the Great Place to Work Institute. Wegmans is the only company that's been on the list every year since inception and has been in the top five for eight consecutive years, holding the number one spot in 2005. A picture of CEO Danny Wegman accompanied the article with a quote that summed up the mindset that makes the company so successful, "The only way to be a great place to shop is to first be a great place to work." I'm quite familiar with Wegmans as I've watched them grow from a small, local grocery store to a regional chain of seventy-six stores and more than $5 billion in sales. In 2003, my company had the opportunity to work with Wegmans' leaders and learn, firsthand, the type of thinking that goes into creating a profitable, great place to work. Speak with any Wegmans leader and they'll share with you the belief about happy employees leading to incredible service that makes for loyal customers.

> If your employees are unhappy, your customers are paying for it.

To fully appreciate Wegmans, you must understand how much they've achieved with respect to customer loyalty. In a recent conversation, company President Colleen Wegman shared with me her experience from the last store opening in Massachusetts. "I just returned from a store's inaugural event and was delighted to see more than 2,000 people waiting for the store to open. Some even camped out! In mingling with the customers, it occurred to me that these people were not just customers, they were fans. Many of them shared with me how many openings they've been to. It was like they were following the Grateful Dead."

Did I mention that Wegmans is a grocery store? If a grocery store with a large number of frontline, hourly workers can achieve ENGAGED status with employees and customers, so can you! (Remember, ENGAGED employees are committed and motivated to act in the best interest of your company, and ENGAGED customers fall in love with your company, are more loyal, proactively tell others about you, and buy more of your products and services.)

HAPPINESS AND EMPLOYEE ENGAGEMENT AT CRISIS LEVELS

Many people are still getting comfortable using the words *happiness* and *work* in the same context. Sometimes they just seem like they don't belong together, like *fun* and *exercise* or *OJ Simpson* and *innocent*. At work, we are conditioned to think about bottom-line results and don't always see the impact happiness of employees has on those results. Happiness is difficult to measure where money is easy to count. Happiness does appear to be closely connected to employee engagement (like a second cousin) and employee engagement is something we have lots of information about.

Employee engagement continues to hit historic lows, which is costing employers billions of dollars in lost productivity and costing consumers in the form of a more frustrating, "I don't really care about you" customer experience. I am not trying to depress you with this information, just painting a picture of the reality. Why should this be important to you? Because employee engagement is directly related to the experience customers have with any company, including yours. Whether your company is in retail, manufacturing, distribution, health care, professional services, or some other unique niche industry doesn't matter. The level of employee engagement has a profound impact on the experience your customers will have with your products and services. And as you will learn on your journey through this book, a lack of employee engagement is expensive!

This chapter shares information on workforce happiness and engagement that may surprise you. Intellectually, you will get it. It will be quite clear what the data reveals and the positive and negative impacts it can have on your company.

As you will see, there is no shortage of research on what many consider the "soft stuff," specifically employee engagement, happiness, and workforce well-being. In the pages ahead I will break down many useful statistics of this so-called soft stuff. You will quickly see that the soft stuff really is the hard stuff to master and fix, but when you do, you and your company can chart a course to greater profitability. If it wasn't hard, then we wouldn't see the same challenges, decade after decade, in trying to get employees to be more ENGAGED and motivated to perform at work.

You will leave this chapter understanding the realities of today's employee engagement crisis and its potential impact on your company and your customers. Most importantly, you will be ready to focus on ways to ENGAGE your workforce with an experiential mindset and ways of "being" that will enable you to ENGAGE customers. And not just because you want to make employees happier and increase profitability, but because it is simply the right thing to do!

LACK OF ENGAGED EMPLOYEES—A TOP THREAT FACING YOUR BUSINESS?

Year after year, I continue to be amazed at the incredible dichotomy that exists between what scholars and researchers continue to report with respect to employee engagement and actions that company leaders are willing to take to fix it. Does it horrify you to know that it was recently reported that 65 percent of workers are either somewhat or totally unsatisfied? Think about this for just a few more seconds. Less than half of the people you work with might claim to be satisfied and happy at work. Gallup's most recent employee engagement study confirmed what many of us who've been paying attention to the continuous slide in employee engagement have known. Even so, it makes it no less scary when it comes to the well-being of employees and the experience we as consumers can count on (or can't count on). According to Gallup's latest findings, 70 percent of American workers are "not engaged" or "actively disengaged" in their work, meaning they are emotionally disconnected from their workplaces and are less likely to be productive. That leaves nearly one-third of American workers who are "engaged," or involved in and enthusiastic about their work and contributing to their organizations in a positive manner. In the article, "Majority of American Workers Not Engaged in Their Jobs," Nikki Blacksmith and Jim Harter from Gallup share perspective on how over the past several decades (not years) researchers have identified a strong relationship between employees' workplace engagement and their respective company's overall performance. This is not new information. Researchers have been hollering this information at us year after year after year. Bottom line: companies with ENGAGED employees witness more positive business outcomes while companies with disengaged employees suffer from lower productivity, higher costs, fewer consistently good customer experiences, and less customer loyalty.

On the speaking circuit in the past year, I have replicated the Gallup findings over and over again. Whenever I have an audience of senior leaders, I ask, "What are your biggest challenges in engaging employees and inspiring them to deliver consistently good customer experiences?" Overwhelmingly, I hear responses that can be themed as "getting employees to care." Do employees in your company "care" enough about the customer and, if so, what are they doing to consistently demonstrate how much they care?

Here is the good news. Executives appear to be more aware and focused on the lack of happiness and engagement issues than ever before! A study from the research firm, the Economist Intelligence Unit, reported that 84 percent of top executives believe disengaged employees are one of the top three threats facing their business.

So why, all of a sudden, is a lack of ENGAGED employees on the "top threats facing my business" list? I'm glad you asked! Research tells us that Americans who have at least some college education are significantly less likely to be ENGAGED in their jobs than those with a high school diploma or less. Additionally, workers aged 30 to 64 are less likely to be ENGAGED at work than those who are younger or older. These types of workers are referred to as "knowledge workers." They typically have higher education and perform more complex jobs that require a higher level of skills and, well, knowledge. In 1990, only 17 percent of jobs required knowledge workers. According to the McKinsey & Company report, *The War for Talent*, that figure has risen to 60 percent and continues to rise.

We operate in a much stronger knowledge economy. Therefore the bottom line is being influenced more than ever by the knowledge worker and the soft skills required of leaders to ENGAGE the workforce.

YOU NEED HAPPY EMPLOYEES TO OPTIMALLY FULFILL YOUR PURPOSE

Remember, the purpose of your company is to create and keep profitable and ENGAGED customers, and you simply can't do it consistently without happy employees. Delivering a branded experience that makes customers happy more often than they would be with the competition is the best way to differentiate and drive customer engagement and loyalty.

A few years ago, I was sitting on an airplane next to a woman from Bain Consulting. She told me about a study her firm conducted that revealed 80 percent of senior leaders believed their companies delivered superior customer service, while only 8 percent of their customers agreed. The study referred to the problem as the "Customer Service Gap." I call it the "Experience Gap," whose root cause is a lack of employee happiness and engagement. A 72 percent gap between what leaders think their customers are experiencing and what the customers actually believe they are experiencing. Is this acceptable? Of course not! In part two of this book, I will cover in great detail ways to better understand the true employee experience and resulting customer experience. You will learn how to quantify your company culture to better understand how to deliver the right experiences for keeping customers and creating new ones.

EMPLOYEES ARE NOT YOUR GREATEST ASSET

For the last six years, I've been speaking to leaders referencing my last book, *Achieve Brand Integrity: Ten Truths You Must Know to Enhance Employee Performance and Increase Company Profits*. When I introduce one of the Truths (like Truth 5: Marketing and Advertising Can Kill Your Brand) I will ask the audience, "True or false?" and they resound with a shout of "True!" I get the same response for nine of the ten Truths. However, when I share Truth 7: Employees Are NOT Your Greatest Asset, something interesting occurs, every single time:

ME: Truth 7: Employees Are Not Your Greatest Asset, true or false?

AUDIENCE: [UNCOMFORTABLE SILENCE FOR TWO OR THREE SECONDS (FEELS LIKE TEN)]

ME: Well . . . is this true or false?

AUDIENCE: [ONE OR TWO AUDIENCE MEMBERS SPEAK OUT, VERY QUIETLY AND IN A HUSHED TONE THAT SCREAMS OF A LACK OF CONFIDENCE] False?

ME: The book is called the *Ten Truths*! Of course this is true.

I can't think of one instance when I've not been able to replicate this dialogue with the audience.

Then I share a slightly different perspective: the right employees who are ENGAGED and performing the experience are your greatest assets. And as research shows, the harsh reality is (and has been for years) that employees are less ENGAGED than ever before. In fact, for three straight years, employee engagement has been the lowest in recorded history.

You may be asking, "What is causing this decline?" I have a few thoughts I can share. During the past few years, many company leaders have successfully decreased overhead expenses while increasing cost savings. But they have also increased the stress and burnout of their best people. In fact, a recent study indicated that 63 percent of employees experience a high level of stress at work and 39 percent cite workload as the top cause of stress. Couple this with the reality that employees have lost friends at work due to layoffs, benefits are waning or less than they used to be, and raises seem like a pipe dream and are no longer discussed at performance reviews. In some cases, companies even fail to do performance reviews (or at least do them well).

In the book, *The Enemy of Engagement*, authors/researchers Mark Royal and Tom Agnew report that nearly one-third of employees lack the resources and information needed to do their jobs. One-half are bothered by "inadequate staffing levels in their work areas." You might be thinking that this is not a recipe for an ENGAGED workforce. Or that this is not a recipe for outbehaving the competition and getting a workforce focused on performing a branded experience. You're thinking right!

There is no question that the difficult economic times of the Great Recession have profoundly impacted workforce happiness and engagement. The numbers speak for themselves. These statistics have been replicated over and over again, and the results continue to tell us the same message about low engagement (see the Lack of Engagement Is Expensive list on the following page).

Lack of Engagement Is Expensive

(Recent statistics indicating the realities of engagement at work.)

- 70% of ENGAGED employees indicate they have a good understanding of how to meet customer needs; only 17% of disengaged employees say the same.
- 78% of ENGAGED employees would recommend their company's products or services, compared to 13% of disengaged employees.
- 75% of leaders have no engagement plan or strategy even though 90% say engagement impacts business success.
- 84% of employees were searching for a new job in 2012. That compares to 60% in 2010.
- ENGAGED organizations grew profits as much as three times faster than their competitors. Highly ENGAGED organizations have the potential to reduce staff turnover by 87% and improve performance by 20%.
- Increased employee engagement was accompanied by a 12% increase in customer satisfaction and significant double-digit revenue and margin growth over the past three years.

Reading this list adds a bit more clarity to why so many leaders are seeing the lack of ENGAGED employees as a real threat to profitably growing their company.

So, if you are still asking yourself if you should worry about the happiness and level of ENGAGED employees in your company, I only have one more piece of convincing evidence. Do the math. What if all employees in your company were EN-GAGED and willing to give the company or its customers five minutes of extra discretionary effort each week? The ROI may astound you, and the improved customer experience might make the difference between surviving and thriving in the years ahead.

I was presenting to a group of partners in a large accounting firm and I asked them to quantify five minutes of extra productivity per day for each of their accountants. I led them through an exercise of factoring in the average salary for each level of accountant (staff accountant, supervisor, and manager) plus the additional employee taxes and costs. Being accountants, they loved this exercise. They tallied up the number of working hours per year expected by each group of accountants. What they found was more than a little surprising. Five minutes a day added up to twenty-five minutes per week, multiplied by forty-eight weeks (factoring in vacation and personal days) equaled 1,200 additional minutes of work per accountant (or twenty hours). They then took the average billing rate for each level and opened their eyes to the dramatic impact on profitability. An accountant billed out at $150 per hour could generate an additional $3,000 in revenue. Another way to look at it is by engaging the disengaged a bit more they could save $3,000 in lost productivity. This firm had over a hundred accountants. We were only talking about five minutes a day! What would thirty minutes of increased engagement and productivity look like?

If you're a seasoned manager, you know that ENGAGED workers are significantly more productive in their jobs. In addition, you know that when ENGAGED workers interact with customers, they are more likely to behave in ways that enable your company to outbehave the competition, driving the experiences that generate loyalty and increased business. How ENGAGED is your workforce today?

THE FIVE LEVELS OF BEING ENGAGED

Where does your workforce, team, or department fall within the Five Levels of ENGAGED?

FIVE LEVELS OF ENGAGED

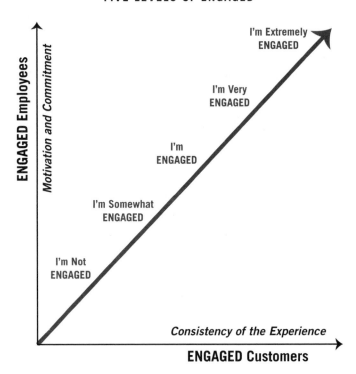

Level 1: "I'm not ENGAGED." Level 1 employees typically have an "I don't care" attitude, distrust management, and provide inconsistent customer service (usually due to lack of process and training), and do not see how they make a difference every day at work. They are unhappy at work and regularly act out their unhappiness.

Customer Experience Result: Bad experience; low retention; no consistency = no loyalty; not ENGAGED

Level 2: "I'm somewhat ENGAGED." These employees may have some understanding of your company's values, brand, and promises made to customers; however, a lack of appreciation and recognition for a job well done helps fuel uncertainty regarding whether the workforce as a whole is really committed to taking care of customers. These employees may not leave your company voluntarily, and in fact, many of them "quit and stay" (ouch!).

Customer Experience Result: Unreliable experience; not satisfied or loyal; low retention; not ENGAGED

Level 3: "I'm ENGAGED." Employees at this level begin to understand how their actions make a difference in the company's overall success. They understand performance expectations and have walked a mile in the customer's shoes, yet they still distrust management somewhat and lack confidence in the company's ability to deliver a consistent customer experience.

Customer Experience Result: Inconsistent experience, which sometimes leads to frustration; somewhat satisfied but still not loyal; not ENGAGED

Level 4: "I'm very ENGAGED." Employees here clearly understand the branded experience being promised. They are focused on what to do for customers and are becoming more committed to performing the branded experience. These employees feel empowered and properly trained on how to *do the right thing.*

Customer Experience Result: Consistent, above average experience; sense of belonging that leads to moderate loyalty; somewhat ENGAGED

Level 5: "I'm extremely ENGAGED (I am an 'experience stager')." These are your star performers who are passionate advocates for your company's branded experience. They love working for your company and tell people about their experience. They feel appreciated for their efforts and are confident in their ability to provide consistent, above average, and sometimes even WOW experiences to customers.

Customer Experience Result: Extreme brand loyalty, which leads to increased referrals; customers here feel as if they are "members" of your brand, that is, a part of your cult following; ENGAGED

WHAT MAKES EMPLOYEES HAPPY AND ENGAGED?

In the best-selling book *Drive: The Surprising Truth About What Motivates Us,* Daniel Pink references fifty years of behavioral science and more than seven decades of research on motivation to overturn the conventional wisdom about human motivation and offer a more effective path to high performance. As the title promises, he shares a few surprises. I found the most notable to be that while we tend to think that money is a prime motivator at work, it can actually demotivate. Yes, you heard me right. Paying people more money can actually be a "demotivator."

Pink notes that the "science is very surprising and a bit freaky. We as humans are not as predictable as you might think." He points out that if you reward employees for things you don't always get what you are looking for with respect to additional motivation. In fact, the research shows that if a job requires even rudimentary cognitive skill (which is just about every job in your company) that higher financial rewards lead to poorer performance. This is contrary to conventional wisdom that the higher the reward the higher the performance.

Pink's video overview of this research is astonishing and can be found at *www.danpink.com.* At the time of this writing, the video has been viewed over 10 million times. In the video, you learn how psychologists, sociologists, and economists have replicated the scenario over and over again—more rewards don't work! More to come on this subject in Principle 7.

Pink says, "Money is a motivator but in a strange way." You must pay people enough to take the issue of money off the table by paying a fair market wage. Once the fair wage is covered, more compensation will not improve their happiness or performance and, in fact, often demotivates.

Pink points out three primary motivators that drive happiness and engagement at work:

1. Autonomy: the desire to be self-directed. More ENGAGED workers are able to thrive in a self-directed environment.
2. Mastery: the ability to get better at what we do. People feel good when they are challenged and able to focus on improving themselves or something they are working on.
3. Purpose: the feeling that you are making a difference.

What I love most about Pink's work is that he presents many incredibly interesting findings that are not new to the world. He does a fantastic job packaging up the conclusions that scholars and researchers have been publishing for as long as we can remember.

Teresa Amabile and Steven Kramer (authors of *The Progress Principle*) present another fantastic pathway for understanding what creates happiness at work and leads to an ENGAGED workforce—quite simply, making progress at work. It has been proven as a top motivator, yet its power is widely misunderstood by leaders. Of all the activities and happenings that can impact a person's mood and motivation at work, the single most important is *"making progress in meaningful work."* Although this may seem quite obvious, it is anything but to most managers.

To prove this point, the authors conducted a study that asked 669 managers from companies around the world to rank the importance of five factors that could influence motivations and emotions at work. Four of the items came from conventional management wisdom: recognition, incentives, interpersonal support, and clear goals. The fifth was "support for making progress in the work." The results of this study revealed total unawareness of the power of progress across all levels of management. Support for making progress was ranked dead last as a motivator and third out of five as an influence on emotion. The concept of "progress in my work" simply is not on the radar of enough managers. Amabile and Kramer noted that across all the companies they studied, only rarely could they identify managers who consistently supported their people in making progress.

Want to improve happiness and engagement? Start looking for ways to help employees understand what progress looks like and make it your responsibility to remove obstacles that get in the way. Consistent, daily progress by individual employees fuels both happiness and engagement, and happy and ENGAGED employees are positioned to make happy and ENGAGED customers.

LIVING THE BRAND SYSTEM

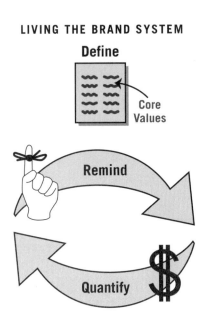

Define

Core Values

Remind

Quantify

CREATING A LIVING THE BRAND SYSTEM TO DELIVER HAPPINESS

From this point forward every ounce of this book will be focused on how to build and manage a Living the Brand System—the one system that touches all other systems in your company, enabling you to manage the employee and customer experience to drive a better work culture and greater customer loyalty. Principle 3 and Principle 4 dive into the DEFINE piece of your Living the Brand System (how to define the branded experience). After that, the remainder of the book will focus on how to REMIND the workforce about the branded experience and QUANTIFY it over time.

Take this wonderful quote by Mahatma Gandhi with you on your continued journey to defining and measuring a branded experience for your company:

Happiness is when what we think, what we say, and what we do are in harmony.

POWER OF THE PAUSE

- What are your biggest challenges to engaging employees and inspiring them to deliver consistently great customer experiences?
- What might be the hidden costs associated with a lack of ENGAGED employees in your company?
- What are the benefits to your company from having high levels of ENGAGED employees?

Don't Just Announce Your Culture, Make It Visible

HIGHLIGHTS

1. Your mission, values, brand positioning, guiding principles, etc., are invisible, unless your employees know specifically how to act them out through their day-to-day behaviors. To do that, employees must have the right mindset to guide the behaviors that bring a branded experience to life. A powerful mindset can be communicated in seven words or less; it is inspirational, intuitive, motivating, and most importantly, easily remembered and repeated.

2. Companies that make the effort to define the behaviors behind their core values or desired branded experience create stronger work cultures that power a more consistent customer experience. These leading companies don't simply announce their work culture or brand positioning through their mission, values, guiding principles, etc. Instead, they truly make the invisible visible with clear, measurable, nonnegotiable behaviors. These behaviors enable the branded experiences that can only be delivered consistently by an ENGAGED workforce.

ARE YOUR MISSION, VALUES, BRAND POSITIONING, GUIDING PRINCIPLES, ETC., ACTIONABLE?

All too often, I walk into a company or pull up its Web site and see the mission, values, brand positioning, guiding principles, etc., proudly displayed, and I wonder what its true intentions are. Is the company simply marketing what is important to it to customers and prospects, hoping to form a positive impression and thus guiding the formation of a reputation in the marketplace? (Key word is *hoping*.)

Or is it trying to create awareness across the workforce of who it is and what it wants to be known for by posting them on the Web site as nouns: *Integrity, Excellence, Accountability, Innovative, Communication*. Well, nouns are not actionable. They are things. You can't build talent and performance management systems around things. It is nearly impossible to objectively hold people accountable to nouns. "Hey, Johnny, can we get a little more Integrity from you this week?" "Barbara, how about kicking up the Excellence a bit more this afternoon?"

The majority of these companies are missing the opportunity to truly make their mission, values, brand positioning, guiding principles, etc., visible and meaningful to employees and customers. That is, to make their brand meaningful. Your brand is what you want to be known for in the market and in the eyes of customers based on the experience you deliver. How different is that from your mission, values, brand positioning, guiding principles, etc.? It's not. (By the way, let's just refer to your mission, values, brand positioning, guiding principles, etc., as your core values or your brand.) For employees, your core values are the important beliefs that power a common mindset—making them actionable and enabling employees to Live the Brand and outbehave the competition. To customers, your core values set the expectation for the experience to be delivered—creating love and making them want to refer the company to others (ENGAGED).

Make your core values and brand messaging meaningful by clearly defining a mindset and making them behavior-based. Begin to think of them as verbs, not nouns. So instead of saying *Integrity*, call it *Delivering Integrity Without Compromise*, or instead of *Accountability* as a core value, try stating it as *Being Accountable for Our Actions and Results*. But you can't stop there. **You must go beyond the names of your core values and determine the actions everyone can and should do. Those actions are the behaviors that power the branded experience.**

BEING A BEST PLACE TO WORK

A culture is not something you announce. It is created by an intense focus on the mindset and behaviors that bring the branded experience to life. This is evident from the best places to work lists that have been developed for almost every industry and geographic region. Take a look at the companies on the list for your region or industry. You will see—they get it. They understand the importance of culture and how to build one that is visible and beloved by employees and customers, rewarding the company with levels of loyalty that are in many cases unheard of by their competition. They understand that culture is quite simply "the way we do things around here." It is behavior-driven, and it is rooted in beliefs that guide a common mindset for employees throughout the company. These companies recognize they can't optimize their workforce culture and customer experience

> "A culture is not something you announce. It is created by an intense focus on the mindset and behaviors that bring the experience to life."

LIVING THE BRAND SYSTEM
Define

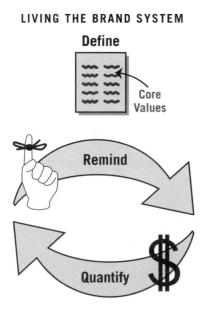

Core Values

Remind

Quantify

by promoting the core values while having a complete disregard for how to actually ENGAGE, inspire, and motivate employees to do them. They realize that without a Living the Brand System, the values become nothing more than empty statements and claims that generate employee cynicism while undermining management's credibility.

I hope you are wondering what it would take for your company to reach best place to work status. In this chapter, you will learn the framework that many best place to work companies use for defining the necessary mindset for the branded experience. Principle 4 will introduce the framework for defining the types of behaviors that take a company from culture talk to real culture change.[1] Defining the mindset and behaviors that make up the branded experience enables best place to work companies to create engagement that far exceeds their competition, which helps to dramatically decrease costs associated with employee turnover, productivity, safety, absenteeism, etc., all while helping their people deliver a more consistently good

---

1. Culture talk to real culture change: going from announcing your culture by posting your values to actually putting your ideas into action, defining the behaviors that make up the desired experience, sharing them with your workforce, creating reminders about them, and quantifying them.

customer experience. Before we dive into crafting a mindset, allow me to share with you a few more insights about being a best place to work from the company that co-created the annual *FORTUNE* ranking.

At a conference this past year, I had the privilege of hearing Erin Moran, senior VP of People from the Great Place to Work Institute, share some interesting findings about companies that are recognized as best places to work. For instance, they tend to have half the turnover of their industry peers. Hmm . . . What would your cost savings be if your company had the right-fit employees, all aligned around a common mindset and then your employee turnover was half as much as your competitors? I also found quite interesting the three commonalities Erin pointed out about these companies:

1. They have better financial results.
2. They have greater trust among their workforce and in management. (This was highlighted as the single most important ingredient to making a great place to work. More to come on trust in Principle 8.)
3. They recognize that the behaviors of management have the largest impact on a successful culture.

Erin also shared critical techniques that these companies do consistently:

1. They assess their culture and actually do something with the data. This is where most companies tend to get stuck because they assess their culture using typical annual employee satisfaction surveys and then they sit on the data, frustrating management and employees alike. (We'll explore how to effectively assess your culture and use the data to Manage the Experience and drive results in Principle 5.)

2. They act on the data collected, taking targeted action to improve their culture, resulting in a better and more consistent customer experience.

3. They learn and share information constantly to keep everyone focused on what matters most and how that translates into a consistent customer experience that makes customers love to do business with them.

MAKING THE INVISIBLE VISIBLE

Consider this: Are your company's core values/brand (or any other internal or external marketing messages) invisible? Are they nothing more than descriptions of potentially powerful "beliefs" that you want employees to hold true? Or beliefs that you wish customers would hold when they think of your company? I find this to be the case all too often. However, this is not the reality for the companies that you love to do business with—companies where employees KNOW the branded experience and DO it consistently. These companies have a Living the Brand System that enables them to get the values/brand off the walls and the Web site and into the hearts, minds, and daily actions of every employee through a common mindset that guides the desired behaviors that power the experience. The mindset is invisible, yet the behaviors and experiences are quite visible.

MAKING THE
INVISIBLE VISIBLE

Mindset

Behaviors

+

Experiences

ENGAGED

As part of the Making the Invisible Visible model, you will learn about three Big Ideas that you can take back to your colleagues to get them thinking differently about the need to define a branded experience and put it into action.

Allow me to explain a bit more about the Making the Invisible Visible method and how to apply it in your company.

THE POWER OF MINDSET

The mindset is the primary ingredient to influence behaviors. Our mindset drives what we think about. It is made up of the opinions and attitudes that guide our actions. Just to prove how powerful your mindset can be, take a moment and think about a recent argument you got into with someone who has pretty set opinions: your mother- or father-in-law, a teenager, your spouse, a Republican or a Democrat. How difficult was it to get them to think from a different perspective?

MAKING THE
INVISIBLE VISIBLE

Mindset

Yes, your mindset is driven by deeply held values and beliefs you hold to be true. This makes it very powerful. Even so, mindset is invisible. This can be a challenge, especially at work because you can't see what others are thinking, but you begin to see their mindset through their attitudes (somewhat visible) and eventually through their behaviors (very visible).

Companies with ENGAGED status make the mindset visible! They get all employees to Live the Brand by first ensuring employees KNOW it so they can DO it!

Last year I had the fortunate opportunity to share the stage at a conference with legendary author and motivational speaker Brian Tracy. Brian spoke just before me (no, he was not my opening act) and wowed the audience as he has done for decades. Tough act to follow indeed. In his talk, he asked the audience to take a moment and think about this question: "What is the one thing you have complete control over in your life?" Dead silence filled the room as hundreds of business leaders sat and wondered. His answer: "What you think about!" Brian proceeded to explain what everyone was very quickly catching on to: the idea that everything seems to be happening around us all day long and much of the happenings are truly beyond our control—except what we think about. Our mindset guides our thoughts. In essence, he was saying, we control our mindset, which powers what we think about, how we act, and how we interact.

Really, what else can you control every minute of every day? Nothing! Your mindset determines what you think about, and what you think about has a profound impact on your attitude and actions. That is what makes creating a common mindset in your company so powerful. Every company has the daunting task of either influencing what employees think or leaving it up to chance. I can assure you, leaving it up to chance is not a risk worth taking.

> ### MAKING THE INVISIBLE VISIBLE BIG IDEA #1
> **If you don't define your company mindset, employees will use their own.**

Here's an example about the power of establishing a common mindset. A woman attending one of my speaking engagements raised her hand and spoke up about her local hardware store. She shared that she loved it there because every time she walked in, an employee said, "Hello, welcome to ABC Hardware! May I help you find something?"

Her story caused the woman next to her to jokingly remark that she *hated* when the employees at XYZ Hardware did that, mentioning that they're always standing there picking their nails or staring off into space while mechanically offering a welcome. "It's just so robotic," she remarked.

This was the perfect setup for me to provide further proof about the Big Idea that if you don't define your company mindset, employees will use their own. I pointed out that the employees the two women mentioned were doing the same behavior, but doing it in different ways—with different beliefs. Different mindsets!

The employee at ABC Hardware realizes that the greeting is an important touchpoint with the customer, and he has the customer experience in mind. He has been trained that ABC Hardware believes in delivering excellent customer service. His mindset is something like this: *Delight the customer at every interaction.* And he's most likely reminded of the company's mindset through communications and constant expectation-setting.

On the other hand, the employees at XYZ Hardware seem unaware of the necessary mindset and might even think the role of greeter is just a function they need to fulfill for their eight-hour shift: clock in, clock out, nothing more. A branded experience may not have been defined and communicated. Or they might not have been trained on the branded experience XYZ Hardware wants to deliver. Or maybe they watched a training video once during orientation where they spent the fifteen minutes joking about the 1980s look and feel rather than listening or learning anything. And I bet managers never check in or reinforce the experience, even if they check to make sure the greeter is at his or her post all day.

For years, marketers have said that companies are like people and that they have personalities. They are right. Wouldn't you agree that your personal mindset is a primary driver of what either helps or prevents you from reaching your full potential in just about anything you do? Marketers say we need to capture the essence of the desired personality and bring it to life. So, if companies are like people, then they too must have a belief system and common way of thinking that brings the personality to life. What does your company believe? What is the mindset that you want every employee to share?

Below are a few examples of company mindsets I've witnessed and read about. I've witnessed them through my own personal experience with the behaviors of the people at these companies. Have you had a similar experience with these well-known companies?

- Disney: Family-fun entertainment at every interaction.

  I was getting on a ride at a Disney theme park with one of my kids. My wife was way back in line with one of our other kids. The ride attendant asked, "Is there anyone else in your family that you would like to ride with?" I mentioned that my wife was at the back of the line with our other daughter. He said, "Let's get them. We want you all to ride together." Why do you think this ride attendant made the effort to find out if our whole family was together and take the necessary action to bring us together? Because he knows that Disney believes that families have more fun when they ride together!

- Walmart "Saving people money so they can live better."

I was a keynote speaker at a conference for HR managers where I met a leader in HR from Walmart. Let's call her Karen. The conference was broken up into two parts with a two-hour break in the middle. After my presentation, Karen came up to me to share some feedback about what she liked about my presentation. After speaking for a few moments we headed to the lobby of the fancy (expensive) hotel that was hosting the conference and where (I assumed) all attendees were staying. I began to walk toward the elevator to head up to my room and I noticed Karen was heading for the main exit. I asked her if she was planning on attending the second part of the conference. She responded, "Yes, but I am heading back to my hotel for now. I was able to save quite a bit by staying at a hotel just up the block." Walmart believes in getting and giving the lowest price. Karen was simply living the company mindset.

- Apple: "Think differently and positively change lives."

Have you ever been to an Apple store or do you own a Mac, iPhone, or iPad? Enough said. You get where I am going. Apple lives it every day!

EXERCISE: CREATING YOUR COMPANY'S MINDSET IN SEVEN WORDS OR LESS

In this exercise your goal is to capture the essence of your company core values/brand in seven words or less. Your task is not to come up with seven random words. Instead, you must create a sentence that makes sense to you and your team and will make sense to all employees in your company.

Don't worry about creating a sentence your ninth grade English teacher would be proud of. Just make sure it will capture the hearts and minds of employees in your company. Consider this your first step in building the Living the Brand System. You are beginning to DEFINE the branded experience.

Define

Core Values

You may find you want to create two different kinds of mindsets. For instance, you may find that you would like to only have a company- or department-wide mindset that guides the thinking for all job categories. Or, you may decide you want to have mindsets for each job category. This exercise introduces a process for creating a company- or department-wide mindset in seven words or less. The next chapter will cover how to create a job-specific mindset.

One more thing to keep in mind before you get started. You are not creating a marketing tagline. While many of the mindset ideas that you generate will sound like taglines, they are for internal purposes only. Keep your internal audience of employees in mind. What is it you want them to believe and think about each day? A colleague who spent many years working for the Ritz-Carlton shared that the company's philosophy is "Don't tell me you are a gentleman, be a gentleman" This same mode of thinking applies here. You don't need to tell your customers what you think, just KNOW the branded experience and DO it.

Do you think you can create an incredibly powerful mindset in seven words or less? Of course you can.

Follow the link http://engagedbook.com/mindset to access the Creating Your Company Mindset Exercise.

The goal of the downloadable exercise is to craft a few powerful mindsets to guide the actions and attitudes of employees in your company and then choose the ones that most powerfully represent your desired culture and customer experience. Reference the Apple, Disney, and Walmart examples above as a starting point when doing the exercise. Here are a few more examples from different industries I have worked in:

Retail

Customers deserve to see us smile.

Not always yes, but how might we?

Welcome, we're glad you are here. (Remember the Enterprise story in Principle 1?)

Health Care

Only together can we truly care!

We are partners in our patients' success.

Recognition and respect are our greatest strengths.

Professional Services

WOW clients with valuable insights.

Do what we say we will.

Strengthen relationships, inspire results.

As you consider the above examples don't for a minute make the mistake of thinking that these company mindsets are soft, or discount their importance. Rather, remember that the soft stuff is the hard stuff when it comes to getting alignment in thought and consistency in behavior.

When doing the exercise, your team will come up with a variety of different ideas of mindsets and more than likely many of them would work well in aligning the thinking in your company. However, you must work together to choose the most important ones to represent your core values/brand

and desired branded experience. I would recommend keeping it to two: one mindset focused on employees (cultural experience) and one focused on the customer experience. Below are important criteria to help you and your team filter through and choose the best mindsets that will have the greatest impact on influencing what employees think about when they come to work each day.

The most powerful mindsets are ones that are:

1. Intuitive; easily remembered and repeated
2. Something everybody should think—every day
3. Inspirational and aspirational; concepts that can ENGAGE and motivate

Remember, a common mindset will drive the necessary behaviors for your company's branded experience. These behaviors will make your culture and customer experience visible. Without the right mindset, achieving behavior consistency is nearly impossible. And as you will see in the second Big Idea, behaviors must be clear and managed, otherwise, all you are doing is marketing your brand.

BUILD BEHAVIORS THAT MAKE A BRANDED EXPERIENCE

If you don't have defined behaviors, you may find yourself stuck with marketing your brand and hoping the workforce will deliver a consistent experience.

In essence, you'll have done what I've coined as "branding for the neighborhood." You've painted the white picket fence, planted a terrific landscape, painted the house, installed beautiful new garage doors, and added a nice asphalt driveway.

You've created amazing curb appeal; your house looks great to the neighbors. What happens when reality sets in? Will your workforce fulfill the marketing promises? If the answer is no, you've probably got some work to do to make the brand visible and create a culture that is intensely focused on

MAKING THE INVISIBLE VISIBLE

Mindset

Behaviors

the right mindset and the right behaviors. This approach to branding for the neighborhood may feel good as you develop new logos and taglines, throw together a glossy brochure, update the Web site, and see your company name and identity featured in an ad campaign. But branding for the neighbors is superficial. You may look great to the neighborhood from a distance, but what if your neighbors come inside? The feel good moments of marketing the brand soon fade away when you are faced with the realities of less than ideal financial results, high stress levels throughout your workforce, increased customer complaints, quality issues, and turnover of a few of your top-performing employees.

MAKING THE INVISIBLE VISIBLE BIG IDEA #2

If you're not managing behaviors, you're not managing your brand.

John Kotter, a Harvard business professor and world-renowned expert on organizational change management, makes the following point, "The central issue is never strategy, structure, culture or systems . . . The core of the matter is always about changing the behavior of people."

Of course it's difficult to change behaviors. That's why so many companies fail to consistently outbehave their competition. In most cases, leaders and employees don't even know what the desired behaviors are. That is why the DEFINE portion of the Living the Brand System is so valuable. It is a proven approach for bringing leaders together to define the mindset and how everyone should behave it. Doing that makes the invisible visible.

Define

Core Values

The late Stephen Covey, author of *The 8th Habit*, wrote about one of the most insightful challenges in our business world today. In his book he stated, "One of the greatest challenges that business leaders encounter is that of working to cascade and TRANSLATE the corporate vision from 30,000 feet into actionable line-of-sight behaviors among front-line workers to achieve critical objectives."

I read this quote and ask, "Why is this so freakin' hard?" The answer: It may be hard, but it's not impossible. Implementing a Living the Brand System makes the translation possible and dare I say . . . easy.

If you as a leader in your company are not willing to define what success looks like behaviorally (regardless of how elementary some of the behaviors are), then don't expect employees to deliver your branded experience consistently because they won't! Expect them to determine their own behaviors based on their own mindset. Remember from Principle 1: all employees are on stage when they come to work. Employees need to recognize this and be ready to orchestrate an experience for colleagues and custom-ers. Establishing a mind-set enables the right thinking that will guide the development of the branded experience and the commitment and mo-tivation to performing it consistently. The behav-iors, and the experiences they power, are the com-ponents of your branded experience that are vis-ible every day, for every employee and every customer.

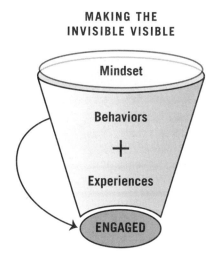

MAKING THE INVISIBLE VISIBLE

Mindset

Behaviors

$+$

Experiences

ENGAGED

Principle 4: Sprint from Culture Talk to Culture Change is all about how to define proprietary behaviors for your company that will Make the Invisible Visible. Before we get into that, there's one more Big Idea.

Is it fair to say that experiences are what really drive per-ceptions about your company? You bet it is. Remember it's tough to disagree with the reality that 90 percent of the time people judge a company based on the experience they or someone else has and 10 percent or less based on the sales or marketing message.

The branded experience is a result of well-orchestrated be-haviors by employees. It is what we witness as consumers of a product or service. As employees, the experience is what we witness day in and day out when we come to work. So, the savvy marketer will appreciate Big Idea #3: The experience really is the best marketing.

MAKING THE INVISIBLE VISIBLE BIG IDEA #3

The experience is the marketing.

In this chapter, you learned about the Making the Invisible Visible framework and the critical first step of creating the right mindset in the definition of a branded experience. In the next chapter I'll introduce more exercises, tools, and techniques for defining basic behaviors necessary for creating a Living the Brand culture that ENGAGES the workforce and customers. You will learn the necessary methodologies by simply reading the text; however, in order to get the maximum value from the culture change tools and techniques most applicable for your company, you will need to do a little work. There are downloadable guides every step of the way just like the Creating Your Company Mindset Exercise from this chapter. By "work" I mean that you'll need to go to the Web to actually get the exercises, learn them, master them, and put them into practice. Are you ready?

POWER OF THE PAUSE

- Are your mission, values, brand positioning, guiding principles, etc., truly visible to all employees?
- What is the mindset that everyone in your company should remember and repeat each day?

Sprint from Culture Talk to Culture Change

HIGHLIGHT

1. Culture change requires behavior change, and behavior change is not easy. There are three types of nonnegotiable behaviors that will take your company from announcing the culture (culture talk) to sustainable cultural change. A clear set of Company-wide Basic Behaviors provides the necessary expectation for how everyone in the company can and should act to enable the branded experience. Additionally, every role in a company has the unique opportunity to bring the branded experience to life through a set of personalized Job-specific Behaviors. And finally, culture change cannot be optimized without managers who are willing to challenge themselves to perfect a set of behaviors that will help them become more trusted leaders.

IF YOU DON'T HAVE IT, BUILD IT

What changes culture? Culture is changed by how we act and interact. Using the orchestrating an experience analogy, it comes down to how we deliver the performance (act) and how we involve other employees and customers (interact) when doing so. Behaviors make the experience visible and memorable. Without them, any hope of a branded experience that creates customer love is simply left up to chance.

Many managers in companies that I meet claim to have "behaviors" to power their company's branded experience, and as it turns out, most (almost all) don't. Instead, what they have are high-level concepts of behaviors that lack specific-

Define

Core Values

ity necessary for a clear, objective DEFINE portion of a Living the Brand System. In fact, based on my research, I predict that only 1 percent of companies actually have clearly defined behaviors that align with their core values/brand. This lack of behavior definition drives the inconsistent customer experiences you and I have every day as consumers. I'm quite confident in this prediction and here's why. For years I have been speaking at conferences where hundreds of managers and executives come together to learn and share best practices. The following is an example of an experiment I've run more than 100 times. This particular example is from a conference of 500 managers and executives.

ME: Show of hands, please. Has your company clearly defined its desired brand image with a mission statement, core values, guiding principles, brand promise, or other way that describes the attributes or associations that you want to be known for? Have you defined "who you are"?

AUDIENCE: [ABOUT 90 PERCENT OF THE AUDIENCE RAISES THEIR HANDS]

ME: Keep your hands held high if you've also documented specific, basic, nonnegotiable behaviors that every employee can and should be responsible for doing.

AUDIENCE: [HALF THE HANDS GO DOWN, LEAVING ABOUT 225 HANDS STILL IN THE AIR]

ME: Impressive. I don't usually see so many hands raised. Keep your hands held high if you've operationalized those behaviors by integrating them into recruitment and hiring practices, employee recognition, and performance evaluations.

AUDIENCE: [FIVE HANDS LEFT IN THE AIR]

ME: Congratulations! You are part of the 1 percent of companies that are consistently Living the Brand every day by clearly setting expectations, communicating effectively, and building a culture of accountability that enables an experience customers love you for.

I have replicated this experiment over and over and over again and the results are consistent. Company leaders continue to live on Hope Island,[1] hoping that the minimal definition and deployment of their core values will create a culture of accountability and lead to a great place to work and more consistent customer experiences. It won't!

> **Documented behaviors that all employees KNOW and DO are the pot of gold at the end of the rainbow.**

Fact is, documented behaviors that all employees KNOW and DO are the pot of gold at the end of the rainbow.

Too often the marketing in the marketplace is filled with lies. Well thought-out messages without ENGAGED and empowered employees acting out the promises made (through behaviors) become nothing more than empty promises with a lot of hope behind them. Culture change happens by changing the way people behave. Anything less is a bunch of happy talk (culture talk). When getting your workforce on stage

---

1. Hope Island: a magical, yet undesirable, place leaders go to when they define the branded experience, then sit back and hope that employees will live it.

to deliver a branded experience, behaviors are what matter most. **Behaviors driven by a common mindset will enable any company to sprint from culture talk to culture change.**

If you are like most companies, there are probably certain behaviors that employees do sometimes to almost never that you *wish* would happen always. To make always (or almost always) a reality, you must (first) document the behaviors and (second) make sure everyone in your workforce knows they are nonnegotiable. Nonnegotiable means that they are required for everyone to do if they want to remain employed. That is, if someone is going to work at your company, these are the behaviors he or she must do because they are important to your company's culture and customer experience.

The box below provides a definition for the three types of nonnegotiable behaviors that can take your company from culture talk to culture change. In this chapter, I will provide you with detailed downloadable exercises you can use with your team to build your behaviors and complete the DEFINE portion of your Living the Brand System.

Three Types of Nonnegotiable Behaviors

1. **Company-wide Basics:** Behaviors that everyone from the CEO to the frontline can and should do consistently. Also known as "everyone behaviors."
2. **Job-specific:** Indicated by the name, these are behaviors unique to a role within the company. They are critical to Living the Brand every day. Also known as "in my job" behaviors.
3. **Leadership/Management:** Behaviors leaders and managers should do that build trust in the workplace. Also known as "leadership/management" behaviors.

EXERCISE: USE THE FIVE DIMENSIONS OF BRAND INTEGRITY TO BUILD COMPANY-WIDE BASICS

In 2008, after many years of working with clients to define their mindsets and behaviors, it was time to take a step back and reevaluate our process. A group of Brand Integrity teammates entered the conference room where posted on the wall were a dozen client behavioral models. We gathered around to review the work our clients had done with us and I asked the team what they saw as the common thread. Within minutes, the Five Dimensions of Brand Integrity was born. It was quite obvious to all in the room that there were five behavioral areas that all of our clients were having success with. Five behavior-based areas that any company—that desires a consistent customer experience delivered by an ENGAGED workforce—would want to get their people aligned around. This was a major breakthrough for our company. Why? Because we evolved our approach to modeling behaviors to help our clients determine the best-fit Company-wide Basic Behaviors in warp speed, instead of beginning from scratch each time.

The box on the following page contains the Five Dimensions of Brand Integrity. We've kept the names generic for a reason. They are not yet turned into actionable statements. We do this because if your company is happy with the existing content that makes up your core values or description of what you aspire to be known as, then you should keep those categories and use the Five Dimensions as your guide for building a thorough list of behaviors. (Keep reading to find out where you can download the Five Dimensions method, which includes a description of each dimension and a sample list of behavioral indicators.)

FIVE DIMENSIONS OF BRAND INTEGRITY
• Culture & Team
• Operational Strength
• Lead by Example
• Products, Knowledge & Expertise
• Customer Service

It is rare that I review a list of core values within a company and don't find at least one of the Five Dimensions missing or combined into something more complex. For instance, *Operational Strength* tends to be left out even though from a behavioral perspective it is something that every company "values." *Culture & Team* and *Lead by Example* tend to be stated in duplicate and sometimes in triplicate. A lot of times this happens when a company forces the use of an acronym. If your company has created an acronym to make it easier for people to remember your values, take special caution to make sure that you didn't force terms together that mean the same thing or leave out an entire behavioral dimension all together. I can count on one hand the number of times I have witnessed a company successfully using an acronym to organize their core values. Successful usage means they've covered the most important behavioral areas without duplication of concepts, which is confusing to the workforce. Beware of forcing the acronym!

" Beware of the acronym. "

You will find that the Five Dimensions is the perfect guide to make sure you cover all the necessary behavioral areas that your workforce must KNOW and DO. These five areas, if done consistently, will ensure you outbehave the competition, thus outperform the competition, and become known for living a consistent branded experience.

In order to build your Company-wide Basic Behaviors—the behaviors that everyone, no matter what the role, should be accountable for doing because they make for a good employee and customer experience—follow the link provided. The goal of this exercise is to craft a set of behaviors (I recommend between fifteen and twenty) that cover the Five Dimensions of Brand Integrity and powerfully align with your values. Think for a moment about your company values. What would it look like to have a specific set of visible, action-oriented behaviors behind each of them? To get you started when building behaviors with your team, I have included a list that you may find quite helpful. The following page contains a list of the Brand Integrity Basics—behavioral indicators organized around the Five Dimensions of Brand Integrity. Why do I call these indicators? Because that is exactly what they do; they point you in the right direction to developing the types of behaviors you'd like to see for your company. You may need to alter the wording or add specificity. Consider this list a tool providing initial direction for crafting the perfect behaviors for your company.

> Follow the link http://engagedbook.com/basic behaviors to access the Five Dimensions method for building your Company-wide Basic Behaviors.

> **If you aren't managing behaviors, you aren't managing your brand.**

Word of caution: Don't let just any behavior make it into your set of Basics. Show conviction to make sure that the most important to the branded experience culturally and for customers make it to the top. There are a few very

Brand Integrity Basics (a starting point)

(Behavioral indicators to use when building a set of clear, concise Company-wide Basic Behaviors. Some of them may work perfectly for your company, some may set direction for the type of behavior you need.)

Culture & Team

1. Support one another in accomplishing their work.
2. Take time to listen to and understand each other.
3. Take the time to appreciate and acknowledge the contributions of others.
4. Demonstrate the culture, values, and mission of the company.

Operational Strength

5. Follow established processes and procedures.
6. Adapt well to changes in the work environment.
7. Get things done in the most efficient manner.

Lead by Example

8. Speak positively about our company and our coworkers.
9. Take initiative when needed.
10. Do what we say we will do.
11. Speak respectfully and honestly with each other.
12. Hold important conversations when needed.

Products, Knowledge & Expertise

13. Share product and service information that helps employees serve customers.
14. Contribute new ideas that strengthen our ability to serve our customers.
15. Support new ideas and initiatives.

Customer Service

16. Effectively handle customer service challenges.
17. Follow up to ensure issues are addressed.
18. Demonstrate compassion and empathy with customers.
19. Ask questions and listen effectively to customers to ensure understanding.
20. Take action based on the wants and needs of customers.
21. Interact with customers in a warm and welcoming way.
22. Identify and pursue opportunities to exceed customer expectations.

important criteria to follow when choosing the best of the best Company-wide Basic Behaviors for your workforce:

Criteria 1: Everyone can and should do it. (Remember, you are defining the Company-wide, "everyone" Behaviors.)

Criteria 2: Everyone can see whether or not others are doing the behavior. (It should be assessable and measurable so it can be objectively reinforced.)

Criteria 3: It must be intuitive, simple, and easy for everyone to understand. (Just like the company mindset.)

The download of the Five Dimensions method includes additional guidance for building behaviors including how to ensure behaviors are not double-barreled (i.e., contain only one idea that is easily measured), how to write them to be action-oriented, and how to avoid confusing qualifiers.

AVOID THE "COMMON SENSE TRAP"

As you work with your team to develop Company-wide Basics and initially communicate them to others in the workforce, you must take precaution. Some individuals may get stuck falsely believing that the behaviors are "elementary." It's easy to fall into the "Common Sense Trap" where you feel that the behaviors are so simple it might be insulting to have to put them on paper. This is a dangerous stance that can and should be addressed immediately. When you have the opportunity to rescue people from the Common Sense Trap, throw them a helpful line by asking:

"Does everyone DO this behavior consistently?"

Of course the answer will most likely be no. Mr. "This Is Too Elementary" will soon recognize that just because a behavior is common sense does not give a company the permission to not document it clearly for all to see. Any company that wants to execute a Living the Brand System needs to get *everyone* to KNOW and DO the behaviors that support the branded experience—even if they seem simple or elementary.

Another great way to get people unstuck from the Common Sense Trap is to have them complete an exercise asking them to rate how important the behaviors are to the delivery of the company's branded experience, how consistently others they work with do the behaviors, and how natural the behaviors are for them to personally do.

Rating Behaviors Exercise

(Three different ways to create urgency and avoid the Common Sense Trap.)

---

1. **Importance:** Use a scale of zero to ten (when zero equals Not Important at All, five is Neutral, and ten is Extremely Important) to ask employees, "How important is this behavior to the delivery of a branded experience for employees and customers?"
2. **Consistency:** Use a zero-to-ten scale (when zero equals Never, five is Neutral, and ten equals Always) to ask employees, "How consistently do others in your work area do the behavior?"
3. **Natural or not:** Ask, "How natural is it for you to do this behavior?" and have employees mark either an X for Natural or an O for Not Natural.

Have individuals share their scores. You will very quickly see which behaviors are most important. In addition, you will open leaders' eyes to how inconsistent the current experience just might be and whether or not they are natural at doing it. It's a powerful exercise. Let me share with you a story to demonstrate the importance of overcoming the Common Sense Trap.

An executive team managing a culturally struggling organization was meeting to review the top twenty Company-wide Basics that were just drafted by a team of their company managers. The CEO commented, "These behaviors are like motherhood and apple pie," negatively insinuating that the behaviors were too innate and of diminished importance.

Fortunately, the managers suspected this type of reaction and came prepared. Before the meeting they conducted a sample survey with managers throughout the company, asking them to rate each behavior on a ten-point scale for importance (how important is it to the success of our branded experience) and consistency (how consistently is it done by employees in your work area). They showed the CEO the results.

Boy was he surprised. Not surprised to hear that the average importance for all of the behaviors was nine or above, but that the average consistency ranged between a four and a six.

The point of the story is that it doesn't matter how elementary or "motherhood and apple pie" the behaviors are. What matters is whether or not the behaviors are important to your success and whether or not you can get employees to realize they are on stage responsible for performing the behaviors for each other and for customers.

> **Can you take your nonnegotiable behaviors from common sense to common practice?**

EXERCISE: DEFINE JOB-SPECIFIC BEHAVIORS

In Principle 3, you learned about the Making the Invisible Visible model and how to create the company mindset. And we just covered how to define your Company-wide Basic

Behaviors for everyone in your workforce. Now you will learn a method for defining Job-specific Behaviors. Think of Job-specific Behaviors as "in my job" behaviors. This method is for the development of behaviors for customer service jobs. This is the simplest, most straightforward job to demonstrate since we are all consumers in daily life. **It is important to note that while the narrative is focused on designing the customer experience for a service-oriented position, this step-by-step method can be used to define Job-specific Behaviors for any role in your company.**

In defining Job-specific Behaviors for service-oriented jobs, you are in essence defining the actions you want employees to do in their specific role to create an experience for the customer. You are designing the customer experience. Every employee has a customer or supports someone who does. That is, every employee is within six degrees of Kevin Bacon away from supporting a customer. If not, then the role is suspect and probably not needed in your company. Designing the customer experience will get employees aligned, ENGAGED, and laser-focused on providing a consistently positive and memorable customer experience.

For this particular exercise, I will take you a bit deeper into each step in the methodology—providing details behind each step and an example of the design in action. At the end of the customer experience design process is a link where you can download the Customer Experience Design method. This download includes all the exercise steps along with additional guidance in the form of talking points and thought-starter questions that you can use with your team.

As you work through the customer experience design process, be cautious that you don't fall into the Common Sense

Trap. What matters most is not the simplicity of the behaviors; rather it's how important they are to the experience and whether your company can perform the behaviors more consistently than your competition—outbehaving them. Also, don't disregard the potential reality that in many cases your customer experience is not as good as you think it is. Remember from Principle 2: 80 percent of leaders tend to think their company delivers superior service while only 8 percent of customers feel they receive it.

Here are the three parts and six associated steps of the customer experience design process.

CUSTOMER EXPERIENCE DESIGN PROCESS

Part 1:
Walk a Mile in the Customer's Shoes

3. Craft the Experience Mindset

Part 2:
Outbehave the Competition

6. Prioritize Processes

Part 3:
Measure and Manage the Experience

Steps:
1. Explore Customer's Desired Outcomes
2. Uncover Experience Obstacles

Steps:
4. Draft Job-specific Behaviors
5. Uncover Above and Beyond Opportunities

Before Part 1, there are three important tasks to get you started. First, you must determine the type of customer you want to design an experience for. Next you need to determine the touchpoints (points of interaction). And after you have the customer and touchpoints nailed down, then you can determine the necessary people in your company to involve in the experience design process. Below is a bit more background on each of these important tasks.

1. **Determine the customers.** You don't want to try to be all things to all customers. Pick a group of customers based on industry (e.g., retail, commercial, distribution, or other industry-specific way), size, type of offering purchased, etc. Get focused on one group or type of customer and design an experience for them. You may be pleasantly surprised at how you can replicate portions, if not most, of the design with other customer groups in the future.

   - When considering your growth goals and objectives, is there a specific type of customer that is most important to WOW with an experience?

2. **Build the Touchpoint Wheel.** A touchpoint is any interaction a customer has with your people, products, or services that leads them to have a good, bad, or indifferent experience. A Touchpoint Wheel houses all the different ways your company's brand interacts with and makes impressions on your customer.

   - For the customer groups you defined, what are the important touchpoints where employees interact with and have the opportunity to ENGAGE customers?

   - Pick the top one or two touchpoints for designing the customer experience (choose the ones that will provide the most bang for your buck with respect to influencing the customer). Designing for more than one or two touchpoints at a time can become overwhelming, making it difficult to implement, measure, and celebrate success. You can always add more later after you've successfully implemented the experience for your first few touchpoints.

   An important note about touchpoints. I realize there are a lot of ways you reach out to and "touch" your customers (direct mail, Web site, brochures, etc.). While these are certainly touchpoints, they are not behavior-based and therefore not the focus for the customer experience design process. When building your Touchpoint Wheel, only document touchpoints where your employees have the opportunity to be "on stage" performing the branded experience.

Let's think of an example that you're already very familiar with. Consider the points of interaction when you go into a restaurant. Assume it's a fancy restaurant.

TOUCHPOINT WHEEL

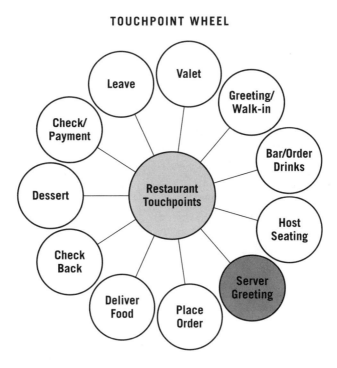

An example of a high-impact touchpoint to design for the restaurant setting is the Server Greeting. It is a powerful, behavior-based, interactive touchpoint. The Server Greeting sets the expectation for how the rest of your experience at the restaurant is going to go. It can have a significant impact in helping you buy more food so it's also an opportunity for uncovering some terrific behaviors that have a direct impact on revenue or cost savings.

3. **Choose your Experience Design Team.** Once you've decided on your customer group and top one or two touchpoints, determine who from your company should participate in the experience design process. I recommend picking individuals who are in the role that will be delivering the experience plus a few other innovative, strategic, and respected individuals. Keep in mind, you are embarking on behavior development of the "in my job" or Job-specific Behaviors, therefore you want to have people on the team who will be responsible for being on stage performing the experience. You may also want to include a few customers in the design process. Or facilitate a separate exercise with customers after you've completed the process with your team to validate your work.

OK, now that we've got some of the initial groundwork tasks covered, let's get started with the three parts and six associated steps of the Customer Experience Design process. At the end of the overview you will find a link to a downloadable guide for even more detail about optimal ways to facilitate this exercise.

Part 1: Walk a Mile in the Customer's Shoes

The first two steps in the Customer Experience Design process require participants to "be the customer" and truly understand what it is like to walk in his or her shoes. Doing so helps participants understand what customers want to achieve at the touchpoint and what gets in the customer's way, preventing them from having the perfect experience. Many times participants are shocked by the power of putting themselves in the customer's shoes. Shocked because they can't believe how many hours each day they provide a product or service without really thinking about or understanding what it is like to be the recipient of that very product and service.

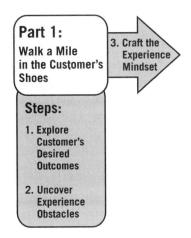

Part 1:

Walk a Mile in the Customer's Shoes

3. Craft the Experience Mindset

Steps:

1. Explore Customer's Desired Outcomes

2. Uncover Experience Obstacles

Step 1: Explore Customer's Desired Outcomes

A Desired Outcome is what customers want as a result of doing business with your company and its products or services. At any given touchpoint, Desired Outcomes become a measure of value in the minds of your customers. If customers receive the Desired Outcome, the experience is more valuable. More valuable experiences have a positive influence on buying behaviors. What does that mean to you? It means that customers buy more of your stuff and tell others they should too.

Using the restaurant as our example, here are a few Customer Desired Outcomes at the **Server Greeting** touchpoint:

1. A genuinely warm and welcoming greeting.
2. To establish rapport with the server.
3. To feel appreciated, as if I'm your most important customer at this moment.

Step 2: Uncover Experience Obstacles

An obstacle is what gets in the way of an ideal customer experience. Obstacles can be ways employees drop the ball before, during, or after a customer interaction. An obstacle may also be something that is out of your control. That is, you or your employees may not be able to prevent it; however, it is important to be aware of the obstacle as you can take action to minimize its impact.

Obstacles are typically a relatively easy list to build. Some of the people on your Experience Design Team are likely the very people who've created obstacles. These obstacles may not be their fault, but because of resource constraints, process challenges, lack of training, or the wrong attitude, they've been a part of circumstances that hinder a consistently great customer experience.

Fault doesn't really matter anyway. Experience Obstacles are going to happen. What matters most is how employees will react when they do. And it matters what actions employees can take to help alleviate the chances of obstacles happening. One of my favorite quotes is from my good friend (and well-known authority on customer service) Shep Hyken, **"It may not be your fault, but it is your problem to try and solve."** I love this quote because it clearly states the necessary expectation for any company looking to create more ENGAGED and profitable customers!

Examples of Experience Obstacles at the **Server Greeting** could include:

1. It takes too long for the server to come to the table.
2. The waitstaff is not friendly or approachable.
3. The server lacks knowledge of the menu items.

Part of the magic in experience design implementation is successfully teaching employees to "watch out" for opportunities to avoid an Experience Obstacle. In addition, Customer Desired Outcomes and Experience Obstacles can also be incorporated into employee hiring, training, and performance conversations.

The most important Customer Desired Outcomes and Experience Obstacles that you uncover with your team provide input for building the optimal behaviors and critical processes that enable a consistently great customer experience.

After walking in the customer's shoes, the next step is to explore the Experience Mindset that will best guide how the workforce thinks about the customer experience and the specific behaviors that will enable them to outbehave the competition.

Step 3: Craft the Experience Mindset

Just like with the Making the Invisible Visible model in Principle 3, the Experience Mindset is a short description that sets the tone for how you want employees to think with respect to customers. It is not a marketing tagline. It must be easy to remember and repeat as it will serve as the mantra to guide the actions of employees.

To make it easy to remember and repeat, it is best to create the Experience Mindset in seven words or less that together make a statement that will influence the way employees think about the delivery of the customer experience you are designing.

For our restaurant, a terrific Experience Mindset to guide the actions and interactions of the entire workforce could be,

"You are our special guest." Again, this is not a marketing tagline but a very helpful reminder that sets the expectation for how to behave.

Now we will shift our focus to the actions employees can and should take to deliver a consistently great customer experience.

Part 2: Outbehave the Competition

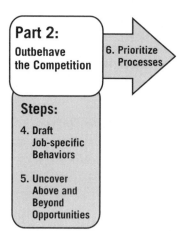

Part 2:
Outbehave the Competition

6. Prioritize Processes

Steps:

4. Draft Job-specific Behaviors

5. Uncover Above and Beyond Opportunities

Steps 4 and 5 of the Customer Experience Design process cover how to build the behaviors that will ENGAGE your workforce and power the experience that will get customers buying more and more often.

When done consistently, these behaviors will enable your workforce to outbehave the competition and differentiate your company. Consistent delivery of these behaviors will increase the perceived value of your offering because they hit on the Desired Outcomes that customers want and also help overcome or alleviate Experience Obstacles that tend to be frustrating.

Step 4: Draft Job-specific Behaviors

Job-specific Behaviors are the actions that should be done 100 percent of the time at the chosen touchpoint. They are the "must do to keep your job" behaviors. Some Job-specific Behaviors may be very basic (e.g., "Smile and say hello.") while others could be more complex (e.g., "Follow up after client meetings with detailed notes and action items"). Either way, these behaviors are to be communicated as nonnegotiable because they make for a consistently great customer experience.

It is also important to note that your team may come to this part of the process with tremendous pride in behaviors they are already doing. Terrific! Make sure those behaviors are documented as well. This step is not about merely creating new behaviors. The ultimate goal is to build a powerful list of Job-specific Behaviors regardless of current consistency.

Examples of Job-specific Behaviors at the **Server Greeting** could include:

1. Introduce yourself by name and with a smile.
2. Ask if anyone is new to the restaurant and follow up with either, "May I share with you a little bit about our wonderful appetizers?" or "I'm glad you've all had a chance to experience our restaurant, let me tell you about the specials."
3. Share what you love about certain menu items.

Designing the customer experience can also lead to the discovery of Game Changers. Game Changers are behaviors that differentiate you from the competition and have a direct impact on revenue or cost savings (when done consistently). These are opportunities for employees to grow revenue or impact productivity and costs in a positive way.

Drafting Job-specific Behaviors is an opportunity to uncover Game Changers. In our example, the simple behavior of sharing information about menu items may very well be a Game Changer for most restaurants.

Your team will be excited by the opportunity to create Game Changers and also highly motivated to implement them. Why? Because the behaviors are their ideas! And because your team will be ENGAGED with the defined customer experience that enables them to deliver what customers want while helping the company either make or save money. Game Changers demonstrate how employees make a difference! And that is important to them! Game Changers help keep employees fully ENGAGED over time.

After completing the exercise with your team, take a hard look at which behaviors have the potential to be Game Changers. Which ones would have the biggest impact if you could just get everyone to do them, all of the time?

Step 5: Uncover Above and Beyond Opportunities

Above and Beyond Opportunities are situational behaviors that employees can do to deliver a great experience. Situational means there are circumstances where these behaviors are ideal to perform and others where it would make no sense at all. Situations can be dictated by a number of factors (who the customer is, the time of year, the weather outside, etc.). The important thing to remember is that the typical employee is not presented with these opportunities on a regular basis and oftentimes doesn't even recognize when they occur. Therefore, it is critical that employees are taught and constantly reminded to watch out for opportunities to go above and beyond and WOW the customer. Just like with Experience Obstacles, Above and Beyond Opportunities are something you want to teach employees to "watch out" for. Most touchpoints have Above and Beyond Opportunities, though there are a few that do not.

At the **Server Greeting**, opportunities to exceed expectations include:

1. Remember customer names and use them.

2. Uncover and acknowledge customer's special occasions (birthdays, anniversaries, etc.).

3. Bring a sample of the special or offer a taste of wine. (Do you ever wonder why salmon is on special? It's because the restaurant has a lot of salmon and needs to sell it before it goes bad. How much more salmon could they sell if each server brought out a sample when greeting a new table? In this case, offering up the salmon may be the Game Changer that helps enhance the customer experience and make the restaurant more profitable.)

Quite often you'll find that Above and Beyond Opportunities can provide some very impactful Game Changing behaviors. The box on the following page contains a few examples of Game Changing Above and Beyond Opportunities. Aren't these outcomes you'd like to see in your company?

Step 6: Prioritize Processes

As you determine and document the Job-specific Behaviors and Above and Beyond Opportunities, you will inevitably uncover a series of processes that are either needed or already in place, but not followed consistently enough.

If a behavior is dependent on a process then the process must be addressed. Otherwise it does not make sense to try and hold your workforce accountable for a behavior or an experience that lacks the necessary process or resources supporting it. Processes should support employees and the physical environment by eliminating service barriers. Employees must be trained to use and improve processes to ensure the experience is delivered smoothly and consistently. Processes should help employees do the behaviors better, not create more barriers.

Game Changers

(Bring the culture to life while positively impacting revenue and cost savings.)

- A delivery company equipped drivers with a dozen donuts to bring to the construction site of their choice. Doing so led to more discussions with site foremen, which enabled increased rental sales.
- A consulting company implemented a process to complete a "How'd We Do?" scorecard with clients at the end of all projects over $5,000. This helped the company gather feedback to continuously improve work processes and led to more work with existing clients, as well as referrals for new work.
- A hospital provided staff with coffee coupons to give patients and other staff members. This kind gesture helped increase patient satisfaction scores, which led to higher reimbursements.
- An insurance company instituted a requirement for salespeople to find three connections on LinkedIn or similar social media sites before going to an appointment. This led to better relationship discussions and referrals.
- A call center encouraged customer service representatives to conduct short follow-up calls after receiving a complaint to make sure the customer was totally satisfied. This led to fewer future complaints, saving time and money.

An example of a process that would be critical to the **Server Greeting** might be to limit the number of tables for each server in order to make sure they are able to provide the necessary time and attention to the customer experience. Or, since one of the behaviors is based on recommending products, another process or system to put in place could be to make sure all servers are able to try the dishes on the menu and, in particular, the daily specials.

Part 3: Measure and Manage the Experience

The Customer Experience Design process enables you to document the necessary mindset and behaviors required to facilitate a consistently positive and often memorable experience (while achieving

> **Part 3:**
> Measure and Manage the Experience

some natural buy-in during the process). The experience that you design will be behavior-based, that is, visible and measurable.

Once employees know the Customer Experience Design and their role in acting it out, then it's time to kick-start the REMIND piece of your Living the Brand System to constantly communicate expectations and hold employees accountable for living it.

While the experience design framework appears quite simple, execution of the experience is anything but easy. It requires a serious commitment to process improvement and a passion for measurement. Remember the recipe for success: 1 percent training, 99 percent reminding. And also, keep in mind, you don't want to make employees drink from a fire hose. Too much behavior modification and process change at one time can kill momentum, frustrate employees, and possibly diminish the customer experience.

SECRET TO SUCCESS

1% Training

99% Reminding

75

Follow the link http://engagedbook.com/ced to access the Customer Experience Design method. To download the Customer Experience Design method use the link provided here. It includes all the exercise steps, templates, and guides you will need to develop Job-specific Behaviors that power a consistently great customer experience.

The remaining four Principles of this book will cover ways to measure and manage your company's branded experience. You will learn best practices for measuring employee alignment, engagement, and behavior consistency in ways that clearly depict an employee's perception of how well they and others live the branded experience. In addition, you will learn ways to ENGAGE customers to understand their perspective on whether they are receiving the branded experience. And, you will discover an amazingly simple and powerful way to make the experience part of the daily conversation by capturing successes and sharing them.

However, before we get into the measurement and management of the experience there is one more type of non-negotiable behavior: Leadership/Management Behaviors.

EXERCISE: BUILDING LEADERSHIP/ MANAGEMENT BEHAVIORS

I would be remiss if I did not hit you with the obvious reality that unless managers are willing to make the investment in becoming better leaders and managers of the branded experience, you can't expect to optimally implement behavior change throughout the workforce. Managerial behavior change is (in my opinion) the most difficult of all behavior change to make happen.

The Leadership/Management behavior model was built based on more than ten years of modeling behaviors within companies. It consists of nine different behavioral areas of focus for any manager who wants to optimize his or her ability to lead. The following model (see box on next page) provides a quick overview of each of the nine areas with a brief description of what each area covers. If you want to dive deeper into an exploration of which behavioral areas are most natural for you in your day-to-day and where you need to focus on improving, download the Leadership/ Management Behavior guide.

Follow the link http://engagedbook.com/leadership behaviors to access the Leadership/Management Behavior guide.

When you download the guide, you will also find an opportunity to participate in a 90-day Leadership Challenge. The challenge is determining three specific Leadership/ Management Behaviors that you can master in ninety days. Simple? Yes. Easy? No way.

The first piece of the 90-day Leadership Challenge guides you through a process of evaluating your strengths and weaknesses in each of the nine behavioral areas. Then you're tasked with choosing the categories you want to work on. Next you build the "business case" by completing a cost-benefit analysis based on the impact that improving the behaviors will have on your life. Finally, you will be guided through drafting three specific behaviors to master in ninety days. That's it—three behaviors in ninety days.

Leadership/Management Behavioral Categories

Behavioral Category	Description
More Questions, Fewer Statements	Being a good listener
Be Respectful	Demonstrating genuine care and concern
Make It Right	Demonstrating humility; admitting mistakes; proactively creating solutions
Straight Talk	Communicating clearly, with transparency, and in a timely manner
Enhance Competence	Fostering learning for self and others
Investigate and Confront Reality	Demonstrating courage in tackling issues and a strong desire to be more aware
Deliver Results	Demonstrating a passion for defining and measuring success
Accountability	Holding self and others accountable
Appreciate and Recognize Others	Capturing and sharing successes; acknowledging others and giving credit where due

Before we close this chapter, remember that as a manager, you have the responsibility to make the invisible visible, ensuring people understand the company mindset (even though it is invisible) because the mindset drives the very visible behaviors and experiences that will ENGAGE customers and the workforce. This sort of culture change can't be done by proclaiming your core values/brand and hoping that employees are going to embrace them and make them part of how they act and interact every day at work. Culture change is hard. And without management committed to Managing the Experience (including changing their own behaviors and holding others accountable to live the company mindset and perform the defined behaviors), it's really hard to have sustainable culture change.

POWER OF THE PAUSE

- When it comes to the current experience delivered by your company, are you losing money because the workforce is not behaving the way you want them to?
- What are the Game Changers that will drive profitability for your company?

PART 2
It's Time to Measure and Manage the Experience

You've just completed part one of ENGAGED. Congratulations! So far we've covered the realities of employee engagement and the impact that it has on the customer experience and your company's profitability. And we've covered a few different ways to define the mindset and behaviors required to ENGAGE both employees and customers. Now you are ready to jump into the execution of the experience with tools and techniques for measuring it, communicating it, and creating a culture of responsibility for living it. As you begin Part 2, which focuses on measuring and managing the experience, keep in mind that your goal is to create a performance-focused culture where everyone KNOWS and DOES the branded experience consistently, ultimately leading your company to become recognized for outbehaving the competition.

Before we move on, stop for a moment and imagine a perfect world where your company has its core values or branded experience very clearly defined. And for your values, you have the top fifteen or twenty Company-wide Basic Behaviors everyone can and should do. You've accomplished the initial step of defining the experience and, in fact, have

LIVING THE BRAND SYSTEM

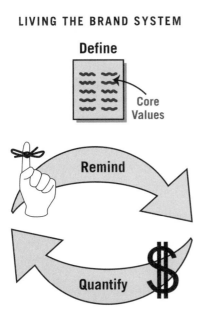

Define

Core Values

Remind

Quantify

communicated to the entire workforce that it is important. You've done the big announcement. You've done the pep rally, but you know that that is not going to be enough. Next you must focus on the reminders and how to quantify the experience. Do you have the image in your head? Great, read on . . .

PEP RALLIES DON'T WORK

In *Achieve Brand Integrity*, I provided an entire chapter on the topic of gaining buy-in from employees. I stated that companies fail in implementing their strategies for one main reason: they don't get buy-in from their employees. They don't get their people to understand, commit to, and take action. Brand Integrity (being who and what you say you are), can't be achieved without buy-in from managers and employees. Your company will never be known for your values (or mission, or brand positioning, or guiding principles) unless managers and employees are ENGAGED with the mindset and behaviors that power the branded experience.

No one wants employees who show up (often late), punch the clock (literally or figuratively), go through the tactical motions to get the job done, and then punch out. But that is what many are getting when their workforce is not aligned and ENGAGED around a company mindset and set of behaviors.

Why do the best employees get out of bed each day to come to work? Not because they are trying to help the top executives make more money and not because they only want a paycheck. No, the best employees want to make a difference. They want to belong to something. They want to deliver an experience that matters.

Pep rallies don't work when it comes to gaining buy in. You've seen this movie before, right? The company has a new set of core values or a new brand promise that it wants every employee to know about and embrace. So the CEO Roadshow begins with live presentations, recorded voicemails, video presentations, Webinars, etc. They announce grandiose plans and explain what the core values are and why you should care. But then they don't have the necessary ongoing expectation setting, continued communications, and accountabilities in place to make it stick (i.e., the Living the Brand System). The pep rally turns out to be nothing more than a bunch of happy talk (culture talk)! It sounds insightful and in some cases quite motivating. However, when you get back to the office and realize that nothing has really changed and there are no measures in place to create visibility or track progress, then naturally nothing positive results. In fact, pep rallies filled with happy talk can do quite a bit more harm than good as employees see it as another example of wasted time and resources along with disingenuous attempts to make positive change happen.

HOLD THE BRANDED EXPERIENCE ACCOUNTABLE FOR RESULTS

Let's change the conversation and start to focus on results. The rest of this book is about measuring whether the workforce is ENGAGED and delivering the branded experience and whether customers are ENGAGED because they are receiving the branded experience.

As you go through the remaining Principles, you will begin to see a 360° View of the experience that includes customer-focused metrics, employee-focused metrics, and the impact on financial metrics that matter most. The 360° View will help keep the branded experience high on the radar as one of the most critical drivers of success for your business and not some initiative that has a start and stop point. It's this type of 360° View that weaves the branded experience into your company culture, ensuring it drives the customer experience as management and employees begin to make the connections between their actions, the customer experience, and the impact on the company. **The 360° View provides the evidence that Managing the Experience is driving a quantifiable gain for your company**—true, measurable results that get the attention of any leader who cares about bottom- and top-line growth.

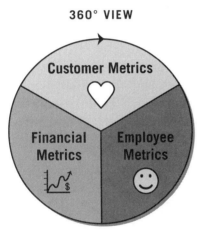

360° VIEW

Customer Metrics

Financial Metrics

Employee Metrics

Principles 3 and 4 provided you the framework for crafting the company mindset and behaviors that make up the branded experience you can communicate to your workforce. Principle 5 covers the employee metrics for measuring the consistency of behaviors and quantifying the branded experience being delivered. Principle 6 is all about the customer metrics that contribute to your 360° View and paints the picture of whether customers are receiving the branded experience. It's up to you to determine which financial metrics matter most when quantifying the branded experience.

The Metrics That Matter Most chart contains examples of metrics that leading companies use to quantify the success

Metrics That Matter Most

Leading companies are passionate about quantifying the success of their business and, in particular, what the impact is of the experience on driving that success. Below is a list of measures that leading companies use on their pathway to more profits. Which metrics should your company hold the experience accountable for?

Revenue Generating
1. Repeat business per customer
2. Average sale per customer
3. Profit margin
4. Customer retention
5. Number of referrals
6. Average sale per top 20% of customers
7. Cross-selling/up-selling
8. Hours billed (utilization)
9. Inventory turns
10. Billing cycles
11. Conversion rates

Other: _____
_____
_____

Cost-Reducing
1. Employee turnover
2. Unwanted employee turnover
3. Quality issues
4. Product returns
5. Employee absenteeism
6. Legal expense
7. Marketing expense
8. Training expense
9. Safety issues
10. Time to fill a job
11. Employee theft

Other: _____
_____
_____

of their branded experience. (See below for the link to download a copy of the Metrics That Matter Most chart.)

In Principles 5 through 8 I will continuously bring you back to thinking about the most important business metrics your company can hold the branded experience accountable for improving. You may even get tired of seeing this chart. Don't. At the end of the day, the metrics are what matter most. If you're not going to prove the success of your efforts or where you're falling short, it will be very hard to keep your managers or executives engaged with efforts to improve the culture or the customer experience.

Take a minute before starting the next chapter to review these metrics and choose the ones that are most applicable to your business. If you think of others, make note of them. Highlight the metrics that matter most.

Follow the link http://engagedbook.com/metrics to download a copy of the Metrics That Matter Most chart.

PRINCIPLE

Quantify Your Culture
to Turn Common Sense into
Common Practice

HIGHLIGHTS

1. Employees who passionately Live the Brand are more loyal and more likely to promote your company and its products and services. A goal of every workforce is to have as many employees as possible aligned, ENGAGED, and consistently performing in ways that enable a branded experience that ENGAGES customers. To Manage the Experience, managers need a way to predict where employees are most Living the Brand and where they are not.

2. Companies need easy and effective methods to measure, learn, and take action in ways that improve the employee and customer experience. A Living the Brand Assessment provides a way for managers to determine how well the workforce KNOWS the branded experience and how consistently they DO it, as well as how to understand the ENGAGED status for any specific area of their company. This short, ten-minute assessment conducted twice a year as part of a company's Living the Brand System becomes a powerful way to REMIND the workforce to outbehave the competition and create customer love.

SAY GOODBYE TO EMPLOYEE SATISFACTION SURVEYS

There has never been a better opportunity to learn the truth about what it is like to work in your company (both pros and cons) from employees. In today's work environment where 65 percent of employees are either somewhat or totally unsatisfied, you better believe they are willing to speak up and share why or why not.

Too many companies are focused on ineffective ways of gathering employee satisfaction and engagement data. Many collect piles of random culture survey data not knowing what to do with it. Others experience gaming activity by managers in order to drive up satisfaction scores. In my experience, it seems like the larger the company, the more this gaming starts to happen.

The following is a story I heard from Courtney, an HR executive at a big box retailer. She shared the challenges experienced with an annual HR survey and how it wasted resources and drove the wrong incentives.

About ninety days before the survey was due to go out, employee-focused activity in the stores would change.

Managers would avoid holding confrontational performance conversations that might be construed as negative for fear that people would score low. They also sent out employee thank-you cards. (Strategically planned out? Yes. Genuine? That's questionable.)

HR was flooded with requests for services like staff parties, training, mentoring programs, etc. Incredible inefficiencies resulted when the requests all came at once.

Managers had a true fear of the results because if a manager's scores went down, his or her store would be targeted, and the store employees would end up in small focus groups talking to HR. Managers would try really hard to keep employees happy in the months preceding the survey.

As a result, employees who had been with the company for a while understood what was going on and took advantage of it. They called it "survey time." It wasn't hard to pick up on why the appreciative events were happening and why some employee behavior that would normally be reprimanded, wasn't. Employees knew that managers acted that way to game the system and drive up their scores.

There are a few problems with this approach to gathering employee satisfaction and engagement data. For one, this approach incentivized the wrong behaviors. Managers cared more about their actual score than the activities truly needed to drive satisfaction and engagement. In addition, the results were not valid. The data was really a snapshot of employee satisfaction and engagement from the last month or two prior to the survey, not the last year.

Courtney said, "They were doing the right things, for the wrong reasons. I could never understand why our company would want to create that kind of a culture."

She also shared that they lost a great leader who didn't want to play the game and opted to leave. I wonder how many more they've lost since then. Culture needs to be something on managers' minds day in and day out. Not just for one quarter of the year.

There is a better way—a much better way. But it requires saying good-bye to the traditional employee satisfaction survey and beginning to measure what really matters most. I won't go as far as saying that measuring employee satisfaction is a complete waste of time. You can make that judgment call on your own. I will say that what you should care most about measuring in the workforce is not how satisfied employees are, but how ENGAGED they are and whether or not they are Living the Brand. If employees are ENGAGED and living it, they are most likely quite satisfied.

A Living the Brand Assessment is a technique you can deploy to measure the workforce's readiness to deliver, commitment to deliver, and consistency of delivering the branded experience. It measures how aligned and ENGAGED employees are with the branded experience and how consistently they perform the company's proprietary behaviors—those Company-wide Basic Behaviors that were determined to be most important to a strong work culture and profitable customer experience.

> **What gets measured gets done.**

As a manager and leader, you will find this approach can create superior visibility as to which managers are making efforts to Manage the Experience and which ones . . . well . . . are not. Consider this: You have to know where you are before you can begin making improvements in your culture. If you don't assess the right things, the right way, then you don't know what the experience your company delivers is really like. If you don't know, you can't fix it. If you don't fix it, you won't reach ENGAGED status.

IF WE ARE LIVING IT THEN WE CAN SEE IT, RIGHT?

Here comes a bold statement. One of those statements that will have you asking, "How could he know this? Does he have four million data points of research to prove this is true?" You don't need piles of research to prove this. Logic will prevail. You simply need to try it.

> **The only true employee-driven measure of whether the workforce is living the brand is the viewpoint of *others*.**

Think about it. The best (and maybe the only) way to find out from the workforce how consistently the branded experience is being delivered is to get the perspective of "others in your work area" and to gather the information in a rock solid, confidential way. Asking for employees' perspective of others they work with is the best measure because it is what employees know, it's what they experience. However, it must be confidential or all bets are off with respect to validity.

A note of caution to those whose work culture is in a toxic stage where trust in management is, to be blunt, nonexistent: You may need to take significant precautions via effective communications to ensure employees trust that the information collected really is confidential. One breach of confidentiality can take years to recover from. You can't expect employees to provide truthful data on whether they feel others around them are Living the Brand if they feel at risk of being turned in or singled out for something they think or feel.

The Living the Brand Assessment provides the most valid indication of current alignment, engagement, and overall behavioral strengths and weaknesses for a company. But, once again, this only happens when confidentiality is preserved.

 You'll find that this ongoing pulse will become a powerful reminder (as part of your Living the Brand System) about the branded experience and the importance of delivering it. Using it as a tool for communicating the expectation of what it takes to Live the Brand creates the culture of accountability all good managers want. You can finally do away with traditional, time-intensive, and less results-driven people surveys and the piles of random, overwhelming culture survey data. Take this example from one of my clients, Linda. She shared this story after taking on a new role as the senior vice president of Human Resources: "We recently hired a consulting firm who conducted an in-depth 'employee engagement study,' which turned out to be nothing more than an arduous set of questions that frustrated our managers and employees. Participation was very low (less than 70 percent) and the results were relatively useless for decision making. We collected mounds of data, and we don't know what to do with it. As a leader in HR I feel obligated to know what to do with this data, but just can't seem to make sense of it."

What Linda shared has become quite typical: exhaustive surveys resulting in mounds of data that HR (and most managers) cannot quantify or compare to key financial metrics. The Living the Brand Assessment approach puts an end to this frustration because it takes the onus of sharing the results out of the domain of "HR only" and makes it every manager's responsibility to review, absorb, and communicate to the workforce.

LIVING THE BRAND ASSESSMENT VISIBILITY METRICS

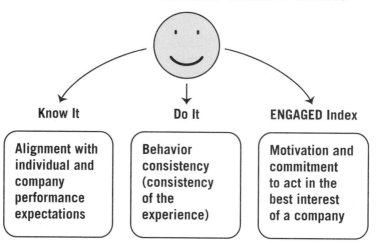

Know It	Do It	ENGAGED Index
Alignment with individual and company performance expectations	Behavior consistency (consistency of the experience)	Motivation and commitment to act in the best interest of a company

The Living the Brand Assessment is made up of a series of indicators that are grouped into three visibility metrics.

1. **Know It Score:** Do employees *KNOW* the branded experience?

   This score is a percentage that measures employee alignment with individual and company performance expectations with regard to company goals and objectives, the customer experience, and whether others are contributing to a strong culture.

2. **Do It Score:** Do employees *DO* (behave/perform) the branded experience consistently?

   This score is a percentage that measures how consistently employees deliver the behaviors that make up the branded experience.

3. **Employee ENGAGED Index™:** Are employees ENGAGED?

   The ENGAGED Index is an indication of employee commitment and motivation to act in the best interest of a company.

Each metric can be applied company-wide and broken down by location, department, and job function. Together they provide the majority of ammunition needed by any manager to REMIND everyone of the branded experience and create a culture of responsibility and accountability for outbehaving the competition.

Let's look at the Living the Brand Assessment components in greater detail so you can see exactly how to apply it in your work environment.

A DEEPER DIVE INTO THE KNOW IT AND DO IT SCORES

Know It Score: Do Employees KNOW the Branded Experience? (Are They Aligned?)

What does it mean for employees in your work area to Know It? It means they understand what it means to outbehave the competition. They understand what a strong culture looks and feels like, how they affect it, and what their impact is on the customer experience. It means they are aligned on the results the company is trying to achieve with respect to the branded experience and their role (no matter how small it may seem) in helping to achieve those results.

The Know It section of the assessment asks employees to rate their level of agreement with a series of indicators that provide insight into perceptions around understanding company goals and objectives, the customer experience, and contributing to a positive culture. Employees are asked for their point of view of themselves as well as those they work with. The score is calculated based on the percentage of people who scored a nine or a ten across each of the Know It Indicators (see box on the following page).

Know It Indicators

(Employees rate to indicate level of alignment with individual and company performance expectations.)

Scale	
Scale 10 Strongly Agree 9 8 7 6 5 Neutral 4 3 2 1 0 Strongly Disagree	1. I understand the goals and objectives of my department. 2. I understand how I contribute to reaching the goals and objectives of my department. 3. I understand how I contribute to a good customer experience. 4. Others I work with understand how they contribute to a good customer experience. 5. Others I work with understand how they contribute to a positive work environment. 6. Others I work with are motivated to go above and beyond what is expected of them in their jobs.

Do It Score: Are Employees DOING the Branded Experience? (Are They Living It Consistently?)

What does it mean to Do It? It means to deliver the branded experience. If your company has gone beyond just announcing the culture and has documented and introduced its Company-wide Basic Behaviors, then of course you'd want to measure how consistently the workforce is doing them.

The previous Principle covered the three types of nonnegotiable behaviors: Company-wide Basics, Job-specific, and Leadership/Management. The Do It section of the Living the Brand Assessment measures the Company-wide Basics—the top twenty or so proprietary behaviors that everyone in the company can and should do consistently ("everyone behaviors"). Often, companies measure the most important behaviors that support each of their core values. For those who don't have those behaviors effectively laid out, using the Brand Integrity Basics from Principle 4 is a great starting point to customizing a proprietary set.

You may be asking, "Why aren't the Job-specific Behaviors included?" Well, they could be, but in many cases they shouldn't be because they are often not as easily observed by others. All behaviors in the Living the Brand Assessment must be assessable. For a behavior to be assessable, employees must be able to see whether others are doing it. Job-specific Behaviors—or "in my job behaviors"—are a great addition to the performance review process. Providing employees the opportunity to rate how consistently they personally do Job-specific Behaviors will lead to insightful and productive conversations with their manager. In regards to the Leadership/Management Behaviors also covered in Principle 4, you may want to consider implementing a 360° Review that asks employees to rate how consistently management delivers the nonnegotiable Leadership/Management Behaviors. Doing so keeps leadership's commitment visible and keeps them accountable for delivering the Leadership/Management Behaviors that support the branded experience.

Now back to the Do It Score. It's calculated based on the percentage of people who scored a nine or a ten across all Company-wide Basic Behaviors. The score can also be broken up by core value, or in the case of the Brand Integrity Basics from Principle 4, the Five Dimensions of Brand Integrity.

Evaluating behaviors regularly is one of the best ways to make them stick and to make sure they get done consistently. Keep in mind the secret to success for Managing the

Experience and sparking positive behavior change: 1 part training, 99 parts reminding. Getting the workforce to assess the consistency of behaviors twice per year and then sharing the information back provides four highly effective and influential communication opportunities. Assessing the consistency of behaviors is a critical component of your Living the Brand System—serving as a powerful reminder.

SECRET TO SUCCESS
1% Training
99% Reminding

The Case In Point on the following page is an example of the power of behavior consistency and its impact on the customer experience and profitability.

The Know It and Do It Scores are valuable data points to infuse responsibility into the workplace for making progress in delivering the branded experience (outbehaving the competition). They make the invisible visible with respect to understanding which areas of the company are living it and which are not. They provide a broad view of how well your people internalize and deliver the branded experience. However, a point of caution when looking at the Know It Indicators or the behaviors that make up the Do It Score: Don't count on just one indicator or measure. No single indicator can provide the whole story or even a precise story of your current reality. This is an important takeaway because it is really easy to get emotional and overreact to any given score for any given indicator or behavior.

Case In Point

Who?
Large supermarket with many locations

What's the challenge?
- A low trust environment was negatively impacting overall productivity and leading to increased turnover
- Misalignment between corporate and store leadership was resulting in communication challenges and operational inefficiencies
- Lack of appreciation and recognition was decreasing employee morale and leading to inconsistencies in customer service
- Employees were struggling to understand and consistently deliver above and beyond service

What did they do?
- Refined the company values and established a more clearly defined set of simple and actionable behaviors
- Increased efforts to capture and share employee successes in order to create a culture of appreciation
- Instituted semi-annual surveys to quantify the culture with Know It Score, Do It Score, and Employee ENGAGED Index metrics
- Created a daily communication with content focused on delivering the branded experience
- Trained managers on how to integrate the branded experience into recruitment, hiring, onboarding, performance conversations, and decision making

What was the result?
Within one year:
- Behavior consistency scores increased across all stores
- Increased sales to top three tiers of most loyal customers:
  > Platinum: 11.3%
  > Gold: 10.6%
  > Silver: 10.4%
- Increased store traffic by more than 2%

That said, there are a few indicators that—when taken together—tell an incredibly accurate story about what is really going on throughout your company or within a specified area. These are the indicators that make up the final metric: the Employee ENGAGED Index.

A DEEPER DIVE INTO THE
EMPLOYEE ENGAGED INDEX

Before I get into the details of the ENGAGED Index, here's a bit of background on the R&D that went into creating it. Of course by R&D I mean Rip Off and Duplicate! All kidding aside, here is how two of the indicators that comprise this metric came about. In the summer of 2006, I read an interesting book by Fred Reichheld (*The Ultimate Question*) about the single most important question for measuring how loyal customers are to your company. It's a basic recommend question: "Would you recommend our company to family, friends, or colleagues?" In his book, Reichheld shares ample research that suggests this question can provide a very accurate measure of customer loyalty. Respondents rate their likelihood to recommend on a zero-to-ten scale. The aggregate responses are then classified into one of three categories.

1. **Promoters (scores of 9 or 10):** customers who will actually refer your company.

2. **Passives (scores of 7 or 8):** customers who probably don't refer you. (Although they may be satisfied, the research says they won't or simply don't refer your company.)

3. **Detractors (scores of 0 through 6):** customers who not only don't refer you, but may actually speak badly about your company to other customers/prospective customers.

In the Reichheld model, a score is provided to help get the company focused on customer service and the customer experience. It's called the Net Promoter Score (NPS) and is calculated by subtracting the percentage of Detractors from the percentage of Promoters. The logic here is quite compelling. By taking into consideration the customers who are not so pleased and less willing to recommend within the calculation, you get a more accurate picture of loyalty. Why? Because the Detractors may be speaking badly about your company and having a negative impact on overall perceptions in the marketplace, which diminishes loyalty. In *Principle 6: Any Monkey Can Survey, Start Building Relationships with Customers*, I introduce how NPS can be used as a part of a Customer Loyalty Index to ENGAGE employees and establish a customer-centric culture that positively impacts the customer experience.

Back to our R&D efforts at Brand Integrity.

In 2007 we began to use the recommend question proposed by Reichheld but in a slightly different way. We asked employees about their likelihood to recommend their company as a place to work and also their likelihood to recommend their company's products and services to others. What we found was quite interesting. First, asking employees the same question with only a slight change did not work well for our clients. In fact, it was quite counterproductive because there seemed to be unnecessary bias that distracted managers, undermining the validity of the results. The bias resulted from some employees scoring one or both questions low because of assumptions they held about whether they wanted to work with family and friends, whether the company would be a good fit for their family or friends, or whether their family or friends would want or could afford to use the company's products and services.

So, after several years of fine-tuning and a bit of real research and development, we cracked the code on how to ask the recommend questions to employees in order to get great insights. In order to prevent unnecessary bias, we included a few assumptions at the beginning of each question. The box below shows how to structure both recommend questions and how to provide open-ended questions to further elicit insights from employees as to why they would or would not recommend your workplace and/or products and services.

Recommend Questions

(Employees rate to indicate their level of satisfaction with and commitment to the work environment and products and services.)

Scale	
10 Highly Likely	1. Assume that a friend or family member of yours is currently looking for a job and qualifies for an open position at your company. How likely is it that you would recommend it as a place to work?
9	
8	• For ratings from 0 to 6: As a place to work, what can the company do to significantly improve?
7	
6	
5 Neutral	• For a rating of 7 or 8: As a place to work, what can the company do to further improve?
4	
3	
2	• For a rating of 9 or 10: As a place to work, what does the company do particularly well?
1	
0 Highly Unlikely	2. Assume that a friend or family member is interested in your company's products and/or services. How likely is it that you would recommend them?

Note: In some cases, additional insights can be gleaned from a qualitative follow-up to the second recommend question. More often than not, insights shared from the first set of qualitative questions are enough for a company to learn what needs to be done to make positive change happen.

The recommend questions help to uncover two critical behaviors companies want their people to do: recruit others and promote products and services. Both of these behaviors are a demonstration of "acting in the best interest of a company." Combining these two behaviors with two additional insightful and correlated indicators provides an accurate picture of how ENGAGED a company's workforce is.

Allow me to introduce you to the ENGAGED Index!

The ENGAGED Index is made up of four indicators. The score is linked to *groups* of employees indicating how motivated and committed they are to acting in the best interest of their company. It is calculated as a net score by subtracting the least from the most ENGAGED employees. The box on the following page describes the four indicators that make up the ENGAGED Index. Each is measured on a zero-to-ten scale.

Using the net score rather than a straight total provides a more reliable view when measuring engagement. It takes into consideration the least ENGAGED employees that can be costly to a company. Employees in this group are often lowering productivity, diminishing the work culture, and prohibiting the ideal customer experience. Ignoring the least ENGAGED and taking the score only from the most ENGAGED group would provide a false sense of confidence. The net score helps managers in making improvement plans that are focused on engaging more people—moving them up the spectrum.

The individual responses to each of these questions are telling and have solid predictive power. Combining them enables you to capture the most complete and accurate picture

Employee ENGAGED Index

(Indicators that measure employee commitment and motivation to act in the best interest of the company.)

1. **Likelihood to recommend the workplace**

   Employees with high likelihood to recommend the workplace are considered committed to a company, tend to promote the company through positive word of mouth, and are hesitant to take a job elsewhere, even in the presence of workplace frustrations and typical company dysfunctions.

2. **Likelihood to recommend products and services**

   Employees who rate a high likelihood to recommend their company's products and services demonstrate confidence that their coworkers and/or the company's product will meet or even exceed customer expectations.

3. **Likelihood to stay**

   Employees are asked whether they would stay with your company even if offered a similar job elsewhere for slightly higher pay.

4. **Likelihood to go above and beyond**

   Employees with high likelihood to "go above and beyond" the standard company practices and operating procedures usually represent the share of the workforce most responsible for giving your company a competitive edge.

The net score is calculated by subtracting the least ENGAGED from the most ENGAGED. The least ENGAGED are those who scored a zero through six on at least three of the four indicators. The most ENGAGED are those who scored a nine or ten on at least three of the four indicators.

of engagement in your company. The ENGAGED Index provides a window into how employees in any individual job category, department, division, or geographic location are thinking and feeling about the work culture, which in turn provides a sound indication as to the impact on the customer experience. It is important to note that the Index is not an indicator of employee performance. An employee who scores in the least ENGAGED group (a zero through six) may be a star performer who is fed up with the work environment or product/service issues. On the other hand, some of the least productive and most unprofitable employees may still score in the most ENGAGED group. You will find that using the ENGAGED Index will spark the necessary conversations to get people on a team, or within a department or geographic location, talking about what needs to happen to improve the score in their work area.

The ENGAGED Index provides managers *directional* insights into the employee and customer measures that matter most to your company. Further, it creates accountability among managers to make sure they are Managing the Experience with respect to maintaining a work culture that is ENGAGED and productive.

For measurement-minded leaders, the ENGAGED Index will become a mission-critical metric that makes it easy to hold the branded experience accountable for results. Whether your company is in retail and wants to compare the ENGAGED Index to average sale per customer, a professional service provider comparing client retention, or a manufacturing firm interested in lowering quality issues, you will find there are many opportunities to connect, compare, and correlate results. Doing so will create the visibility between how ENGAGED employees are and the impact on financial results. For example, I recently received an unsolicited email from Bryan, the COO of a large bank, who said, "We are finding it quite interesting that our ENGAGED Index seems to correlate with loan production throughout our branches." He went on to share how the bank has been focusing on loan sales as part of their growth strategy and that the ENGAGED Index has helped create visibility as to which areas of the bank are focused on executing the strategy and which areas need even more reminding. This is a great example of leadership holding the work culture and associated branded experience accountable for business results.

Two important questions to ask yourself: How ENGAGED are you at work? How ENGAGED are others in your company? At the end of this Principle, you will find a link to access a simple, easy-to-share measurement of ENGAGED. You can then tie this ENGAGED metric to the other measures that matter most to your company (see the Metrics That Matter Most chart on the following page).

VISIBILITY CREATES ACCOUNTABILITY

Managers love the Know It Score, Do It Score, and ENGAGED Index visibility metrics that the Living the Brand Assessment provides. Not just because they are easy to calculate and understand. They also love them because:

1. **They're Emotional and Action-oriented**
   - The metrics provide actionable business intelligence into how well a company is making progress (or not) in building an aligned and ENGAGED work culture that enables the desired customer experience.
   - The simplicity of the metrics wins advocates and converts skeptics (with respect to typical employee satisfaction and culture surveys) by enabling easier alignment throughout the company. They are not complicated and all managers can easily become ENGAGED and motivated by them.

Metrics That Matter Most

Which metrics should you hold the experience accountable for?

Revenue Generating	Cost-Reducing
1. Repeat business per customer	1. Employee turnover
2. Average sale per customer	2. Unwanted employee turnover
3. Profit margin	3. Quality issues
4. Customer retention	4. Product returns
5. Number of referrals	5. Employee absenteeism
6. Average sale per top 20% of customers	6. Legal expense
7. Cross-selling/up-selling	7. Marketing expense
8. Hours billed (utilization)	8. Training expense
9. Inventory turns	9. Safety issues
10. Billing cycles	10. Time to fill a job
11. Conversion rates	11. Employee theft
Other:	Other:

- All employees can understand what the numbers mean and they reinforce what the company is trying to achieve—more growth with great people who are willing and likely to do what it takes to outbehave the competition and make the company more successful.

- Each metric gives managers insight into the key areas of focus for improving the employee experience, which directly influences the customer experience.

2. **They're Quantifiable and Enable Decision Making**

- They link directly to cost-reduction, cost-avoidance, employee productivity, and revenue metrics.

- When compared to customer satisfaction, loyalty, and retention data, they can provide great insights to guide confident decisions.

The following Case In Point highlights an example of how a leading company creates visibility for all managers and employees with respect to the impact of an ENGAGED workforce on company costs and revenue growth. Is there

---

Case In Point

Who?
Large regional accounting firm

What's the challenge?
- Significant company expansion made it difficult to create desired visibility of employees delivering the experience behind the values
- Unable to get employees and leadership aligned and ENGAGED with the optimal culture for the future
- Struggling to help firm members see the importance and urgency around growth

What did they do?
- More clearly defined the desired company culture with a set of simple and actionable behaviors
- Implemented an employee recognition program focused on the values in action
- Instituted semi-annual surveys to quantify the culture with Know It Score, Do It Score, and Employee ENGAGED Index metrics

What was the result?
- 29 point increase in ENGAGED Index over two years
- 92% decrease in unwanted employee turnover and 58% drop in total turnover over three years
- 17% increase in revenue per billable employee over three years
- 15% increase in revenue per all full-time employees over three years

---

an argument here for perfect correlation? Of course not. However, the act of comparing these metrics to show interesting trends becomes a powerful reminder about the branded experience and the importance of outbehaving the competition.

HOW ENGAGED IS YOUR WORKFORCE?

The Living the Brand Assessment is another critical piece of your Living the Brand System. When conducted regularly, it fuels management's ability to REMIND employees about the branded experience and reinforce that they are on stage delivering it every day. The results provide managers with the data needed to QUANTIFY the experience, tie to key financial metrics, and monitor improvements and areas of focus over time.

LIVING THE BRAND SYSTEM

Take a moment and think about the employees in your work area. How ENGAGED are they? How ENGAGED are you? In Principle 2, you learned about the Five Levels of EN-GAGED. Building on the five levels, you can use the Know It and Do It Scores and the ENGAGED Index to quickly segment

FIVE LEVELS OF ENGAGED

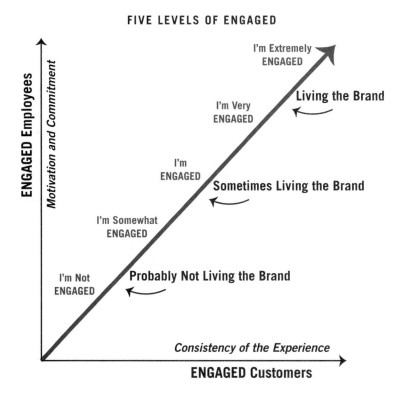

groups of coworkers into three categories based on whether they are Living the Brand.

1. **Living the Brand (very ENGAGED to extremely ENGAGED):** These employees are advocates for your company, helping to find future talent. They tend to speak positively about your company's offerings, leading to increased sales. They go above and beyond when called upon and often look for opportunities to do so. These employees plan to stay with your company. Your goal should be to create as many ENGAGED employees as possible. Why? Because you like working with them and so do others. And, they are more profitable employees.

2. **Sometimes Living the Brand (somewhat ENGAGED to ENGAGED):** Employees in this category demonstrate inconsistent attitudes and actions that sometimes make work stressful, drain productivity, and lead to inconsistent customer experiences that minimize customer loyalty. However, at other times they seem ENGAGED, are more positive about work, and might even share their positivity with others. The unpredictability of these employees can drive you and your colleagues crazy. More times than not, they will support your company even if they seem a bit indifferent. Your goal is to move these employees up to ENGAGED.

3. **Probably Not Living the Brand (not ENGAGED to somewhat ENGAGED):** This group can include star performers who are at risk of leaving or becoming unproductive because they are tired of picking up the slack for nonperformers or frustrated with the work environment or product/service issues. Even worse, these can be your nonperformers whose mindset and behaviors are toxic to the work culture and lead to consistently bad customer experiences. Either way, these employees in general are most likely to be the creators of stress in the work environment. Your goal should be to move them up to a higher ENGAGED level or move them out of your company.

FIND OUT HOW ENGAGED YOUR WORKFORCE IS

Leading companies know how ENGAGED their workforce is and are focused on improving it. With employee engagement levels at crisis proportions, you can't just sit back, remain idle, and continue to allow the negative impact on productivity and employee morale to deteriorate the customer experience. Even if you feel your company's workforce is highly

ENGAGED and is only witnessing the occasional inconsistent customer experience, the consequences may be too costly.

Here is what I suggest you do. Before taking on the entire Living the Brand Assessment presented in this chapter, find out the truth about how ENGAGED your company's workforce is. If you believe your ENGAGED level is high, prove it and celebrate your success. However, if you feel that your workforce is not as ENGAGED as you would like, it may be time to create a sense of urgency to make positive change happen.

Get the conversation going about your company's EN-GAGED status. Find out where your company stands compared to others in your industry. See how you compare to other leading (and struggling) companies across the country.

How? Simple.

Access the ENGAGED Index survey. In less than twenty seconds, you can share your personal perspective on how EN-GAGED you are. You'll then have the opportunity to see the global ENGAGED Index and your company's ENGAGED Index.

> Follow the link http://engagedbook.com/engaged index to access the ENGAGED Index.

It's easy, anonymous, and free! And better yet, it's a great way to spark the conversations necessary to bring your company closer to improving your culture, quantifying your culture, and improving the customer experience.

At this point you may be thinking, "All of this is great for understanding and sustaining/increasing the level of EN-GAGED employees within my company, but how do I know if my customers are ENGAGED?"

I say to you, "Read on . . ."

POWER OF THE PAUSE

- How ENGAGED are employees in each department or location?
- Which managers are most effective at leading an ENGAGED workforce? Which ones are not?
- What is the impact of employee engagement on sales, customer retention, or other revenue-generation or cost-reduction measures?

Any Monkey Can Survey, Start Building Relationships with Customers

---

HIGHLIGHTS

1. In this day and age, you have access to a plethora of technology and tools that allows the automation needed to do amazing things with respect to connecting with customers. But that doesn't mean you should use it to annoy customers with survey requests.

2. Having Quality Conversations with customers enables you to learn firsthand about when your company is Living the Brand and out-behaving the competition (and when it is not). If you play your cards right, a healthy customer relationship and a well-planned conversation will enable you to get referrals that drive more sales. The two most important questions you can ask your customers are "What else can we do for you?" and "Who else do you know that would benefit from the experience we deliver?"

3. Every senior leader would like to have stronger customer relationships that lead to more cross-selling, up-selling, issue resolution, and referrals without having to incur the time-intensive cost of reaching out to customers, conversing with them, learning from them, and sharing information back with the workforce. It is a big investment of time to converse with customers, and many companies do not have the right program or approach in place. And many managers lack the awareness that a well-executed program actually drives bottom-line results.

ALMOST ALL COLLECT FEEDBACK. FEW USE IT TO IMPROVE AND GROW

In this chapter you will learn a simple and practical approach for reaching out to customers, inviting them to give you feedback in ways that will ENGAGE (not annoy) and provide your company an opportunity to increase retention and grow sales.

> "Customers referring you to friends, family, or colleagues is way more powerful than any advertising you could ever do."

We are all busy at work. We're glued to our computer screens or mobile phones and mired in the daily tasks of getting work done. There are simply not enough hours in the day, so only the urgent tends to get addressed. Is this the reality you face week in and week out? You, like so many others, may be missing the opportunity to connect with customers. I'm continuously amazed how easy it is to move "interacting with customers, learning from them, and taking action on results" to the bottom of the priority list. It's true. I've done it and you probably have too. I find this interesting since connecting with customers enables our company (and yours) to fulfill its purpose (create and keep more profitable and ENGAGED customers).

When speaking to an audience of senior leaders, I routinely ask, "Is there anyone here whose company would not benefit greatly from having managers reach out and speak to two customers each week, just to learn how their experience has been? Please raise your hand if your company would not benefit from such activity." Rarely does a hand go up. You can hear crickets while the audience contemplates the reality that if they reached out to customers more to converse and connect with them, they would build stronger relationships, fix broken processes, and ultimately drive significant revenue growth.

Sending out a survey is easy. Inviting customers to give feedback and then effectively following up to uncover opportunities is much more difficult. This is why such a small percentage of companies do it. It's just not natural for managers to proactively call customers and have a conversation about the experience. And because it's uncomfortable, most simply won't do it even though research clearly shows the importance of "closing the loop."

According to research by callcentres.net, 95 percent of companies collect feedback from their customers, yet only 10 percent actively follow up to do something about it. Another study reported that only 5 percent report back to customers that they acted on the feedback provided, and 69 percent of companies don't share customer feedback with their customer-facing people. Ugh . . . makes you wonder why companies even bother to reach out and ask customers for their opinions in the first place!

In 2012, the Temkin Group reported that only 33 percent of companies use customer experience metrics to inform business decisions. How can this be? Why aren't more managers using customer data to make strategic decisions? Here lies the answer. While managers know they have challenges managing the customer experience, there's a gap between what they know and their willingness to devote resources or make the investment to do something about it. In fact, a study from the Customer Management Exchange Network reported that 61 percent of leaders cite customer experience management as their greatest challenge. It is a big investment of time to converse with customers, and many companies do not have the right program or approach in place. And many managers lack the awareness that a well-executed program actually drives bottom-line results.

My goal in this Principle is to share an easy-to-execute approach that clearly shows a path to quantifiable results. But before I take you there, let's first acknowledge the reality of what is happening in the marketplace today with respect to soliciting customer feedback.

WHY BOMBARDMENT HAPPENS AND WHY IT'S GETTING WORSE

In the market today there is an abundance of technologies that make it convenient and easier than ever to survey customers. The accessibility is nice, and companies are taking advantage of it (as my email inbox can certainly confirm). Unfortunately, bombarding customers with a seemingly endless list of questions using overly simple, yet affordable, survey tools has become a popular way for companies to connect. I find it annoying when I'm trying to purchase something online that I can't get to my shopping cart without a pop-up asking me to take a survey. Or when I'm on the phone and before I can talk to a live person, an automated voice asks if I'd be willing to receive a callback survey afterward. And, even worse, when I take my receipt from the cashier at a large sporting goods chain and he pesters me to complete the survey he's circled on the receipt, jokingly saying, "If you score me well, I get to keep my job and pay my rent this month."

Recently I was speaking with a group of leaders when one of them shared a story that reinforced my point. He talked about a recent car buying experience, where the salesman offered to give him a $75 gas card if he promised to rate the sale all fives on the car manufacturer survey he would receive within a week of the purchase. So I asked him if he took the card. He did. Then I asked if he rated all fives. He said that he felt like he had to since he took the card. Now the definition of a bribe is "anything given or serving to persuade or induce." I'm just saying.

What kind of data do you think these companies are getting? I'll tell you. Useless data! Why is it useless? Because managers have no idea how to use it to ENGAGE customers. It can't be valid data if customers are coerced or forced into giving it. And it's not strengthening relationships or driving sales. Surveying must be done the right way, and bombarding customers in a selfish act to "learn" from them is not the answer.

> **What could be worse than doing a survey? Not doing anything productive with the results!**

Here is my take on the root cause of the survey bombardment issue: misaligned incentives. Rarely is there a mid- to large-sized company that does not have a strategic initiative in place to learn more about their customers. (Marketing personnel everywhere feel pressure from leadership to get the VOC—"voice of the customer.") But most consumers (B2B and B2C) feel overwhelmed with requests from companies for feedback. And many times, they just don't want to give it. According to a recent study reported in *Loyalty Management*, response rates from traditional forms of feedback (surveys, comment cards, inbound emails, Web site comments, and call-ins) is on the decline, falling from 50 percent in 2007 to 28 percent in 2011.

These days, it's so easy to reach out to customers. In addition to the variety of survey tools, the great majority of customers are plugged in to email, text, Facebook, LinkedIn, Twitter, and other social media outlets. The same study reported that as traditional feedback volume decreased, per store per year mentions on social feedback channels grew exponentially, skyrocketing from 450 to 9,330.

It makes sense to go where your customers are. If customers are turning to Facebook, blogs, and Twitter to voice their opinions, then companies should respond by using those channels to diffuse problems and try to create more positive perceptions and word of mouth. But in addition to that, companies who are interested in learning how ENGAGED and loyal their customers are and measuring it over time should consider a more intimate and focused approach for connecting and building strong relationships. An approach that does not randomly ask every tenth online shopper or customer support phone caller for feedback on their experience, knowing that not only do most absolutely NOT want to participate, but also because it results in immense amounts of data that become more and more invalid year after year.

A 2011 Global CMO Strategy survey stated that 70 percent of marketers say they feel incapable of analyzing and responding to the glut of data available about their consumers. I realize marketers are in a tough position as they continue to learn ways to control or at least manage the social media channels, scouring for opportunities to make sense of the feedback and proactively react. But you don't need a glut of data. You just need enough data to spark a Quality Conversation. Marketers and managers have an amazing opportunity to reach out to customers, converse with them, and learn about their experience. **You might be pleasantly surprised at how easily you can delight customers by showing them how much you truly care.**

Read on to learn a better way to collect, listen to, learn from, and act on customer feedback—an approach that is operationally driven and enables engagement with customers through minimal data collection and an abundance of Quality Conversations.

ASKING "WHAT ELSE? WHO ELSE?"

In *Principle 5: Quantify Your Culture to Turn Common Sense into Common Practice*, I mentioned how Fred Reichheld and his book *The Ultimate Question* were the inspiration for my company to include Recommend It within our Living the Brand Assessment. When it comes to customers, the recommend question supported by Reichheld and many others is a great way to get insight into the customer experience; however, it is not enough on its own.

Think about it. What good does it do if a customer recommends your company ten times if zero of those ten recommendations turns into a sale? You should strive to be intentional about customer promotion. Two studies conducted with firms in the telecommunication and financial services industries show that only about 10 percent of Promoters (the respondents most likely to recommend the company to others) actually do bring in profitable new customers. That's not bad, of course, but what about the other 90 percent? Why not intentionally provide opportunities to your Promoters and invite them to, you know, promote you? What you really want from customers is the ultimate compliment: the referral.

A referral requires more effort and it comes from a stronger relationship. Consider the difference: In a conversation with my friend Doug, I learn that he is looking for a good advisor to help with financial investments. I have an associate (Melissa) at a firm that would be a perfect fit for Doug's needs. I am happy to make the introduction and recommend Melissa's firm to him. Doug may or may not reach out to Melissa, despite my recommendation. On the other hand, I could send an email to both Doug and Melissa introducing them and suggesting that they would benefit from meeting. That little gesture takes the situation well beyond a simple recommendation that in most cases wouldn't come to fruition. Or, even better, I could call up Doug to say that I'm having lunch with Melissa on Friday and invite him to come. Now that's a very powerful referral! I've demonstrated that I'm a loyal customer by moving beyond a recommendation to a referral and hopefully scored Melissa some new business while helping out a friend.

> **Earn the right to ask 'What Else? Who Else?'**

Having coversations with customers and asking them *what else* you can do for them or *who else* they might know that would benefit from the company's products and services is not a natural act. The average manager has a very hard time picking up the phone to ask these questions and quite often shies away from asking when in person. However, more times than not your customers are really happy with the experience they are having (or you wouldn't be in business) and would be willing to make a referral. When you follow up with customers to learn what it is that they like about your company, or what you can do to fix a problem they have shared, it gives you the permission to say, "Glad you're happy Mr. Customer, what else can we do for you?" or "Who else do you know that could benefit from the type of value you receive from your experience with us?"

How might managers in your company start conversations with your customers that position them to ask "What Else" and "Who Else"?

QUALITY CONVERSATIONS DRIVE RESULTS

One of the greatest benefits of conversing with customers and learning from and sharing their feedback is that doing so motivates action and drives revenue. Traditional customer satisfaction research is anonymous and misses the opportunity to establish two-way communication with customers. In addition, the tactics are becoming more and more unacceptable as we as consumers won't (and shouldn't) tolerate constant surveying with little-to-no follow-up action. If the commitment to earning customer loyalty is not a top priority for your company and is not something that can be supported from the top down, then the following approach may not be for you. If, however, you want to stop the illusion of customer focus and instead demonstrate that you truly care about their experience and are willing to invest in meaningful and growth-focused Quality Conversations, read on. You're about to learn about ways to connect with customers that will drive three powerful results.

ENGAGED Customers Help Your
Company Fix, Share, and Ring!

1. **Fix a problem.** Uncover operational cost savings or rescue potentially lost customers.

2. **Share successes and challenges.** Bring employees into the loop. Helping them understand customer feedback reinforces their role in delivering the branded experience and gets them more ENGAGED and focused on outbehaving the competition.

3. **Ring the cash register.** All companies have a register to ring. You can ring it more if you can achieve more up-sell and cross-sell opportunities, or get more referrals to new customers. This happens through conversing more with customers.

What I am about to share with you is not a research approach. Instead, it is a reliable program based on the philosophy that your customers don't want to be bombarded with surveys but do want a relationship with your company and want their feedback taken seriously. Especially since customers know they are doing YOU the favor by providing feedback. There is a significant difference between what I call a "monkey" survey and a program focused on driving Quality Conversations. For starters, any monkey can lay out questions of various types and invite thousands of customers to participate.

> The quality of your program will be directly correlated to the quality of the conversations you have with customers.

To have a program that will help your company Fix, Share, and Ring you must have:

1. A short set of questions
2. A small, yet very targeted, segment of customers

3. A disciplined follow-up approach focused on Quality Conversations and asking "What Else? Who Else?"

4. A well laid out plan for following up with customers to spark Quality Conversations (Note that this is the part of the process where many companies fall flat. Don't underestimate the time commitment necessary to follow up with customers who are on their own schedules.)

What you learn from customers will help your company to operationally improve. In addition, the program provides an incredible communication engine to help ENGAGE employees. (Remember, 69 percent of companies do not share customer feedback with the individuals who are actually delivering the customer experience!)

Your ultimate goal is to create an ENGAGED customer. The approach you are about to read about will take your company from simply surveying and collecting data to Managing the Experience your customers have and quantifying it in a way that drives the success of your business. You are about to learn about a Customer Engagement Program that enables you to spark Quality Conversations.

BUILD RELATIONSHIPS WITH A CUSTOMER ENGAGEMENT PROGRAM

In most cases, the ultimate goal in surveying customers should be to create ENGAGED customers more than to collect data for analysis. Why? Because an ENGAGED customer rewards your company with:

1. Retention: they keep doing business with you, buying your stuff

2. Advocacy: they tell others to do business with your company—sometimes as a recommendation and sometimes, even better, as a referral

A program focused on engaging customers is simple in concept: invite customers to participate, start the conversation, learn from them, and act on their feedback. However, implementing a successful program (as with any program) requires an initial investment to design it in a way that will meet your company's needs as well as significant investment in relationship-building time with customers.

Of course, every senior leader would like to have stronger customer relationships that lead to more cross-selling, up-selling, issue resolution, and referrals without having to incur the time-intensive cost of reaching out to customers, conversing with them, learning from them, and sharing information back with the workforce. But that's not the reality. There is a big economic trade-off between the cost of following up strategically and effectively with customers and the process improvements and revenue growth that can result. If done correctly, a Customer Engagement Program will allow for Quality Conversations, leading to enriched relationships and easily identifiable ROI. For example, Apple has reported that for every hour their employees spend following up with "not satisfied" customers, they generate $1,000 in additional sales within six months. Not a bad hourly sale rate! And these are the less-than-happy customers.

So let's review the process. The following section dives into a high-level view of what makes up a successful Customer Engagement Program.

CUSTOMER ENGAGEMENT PROGRAM PROCESS

1. **Invite:** The success of a Customer Engagement Program doesn't come from getting out tons of surveys. Success comes from following up with as many customers as you can to have conversations and build relationships. You are inviting customers to give you feedback on their experience for mutual benefit. You are learning and acting on what customers tell you to help improve the experience you deliver. You are not just surveying customers! One more thing about the Invite—while it may be ideal to gather feedback from many customers, it's more important to begin with the customers you care most about. A well-designed program should target the customers you most want to ENGAGE and grow.

2. **Converse:** Every customer who responds to your invite is now providing you an opportunity to start a conversation where you can learn about his or her experience, show appreciation and thanks, and/or take action in some way. Most importantly, when conversing with customers you have the opportunity to Fix an issue, Share a success or challenge, and Ring the register. Be realistic about the amount of investment you will make in following up. Will ten

different managers need to spend three hours a week for one month? If so, make sure those managers know they need to invest the time as this is where most programs fall apart and fail to deliver results. The follow-up conversation must happen if you want to see the ongoing results of a more ENGAGED workforce, operational process improvements, and the ultimate benefits of increased sales and referrals (ENGAGED customers).

Follow the link http://engagedbook.com/quality conversations to access a guide for conducting Quality Conversations.

3. **ENGAGED Employees:** One of the best ways to create more ENGAGED employees is to help them understand the impact they have on the lives of others and on the success of your company. I recently read an article in *Harvard Business Review* about the importance of connecting employees to the end user. The article states that doing so drives motivation, productivity, and satisfaction because of three mechanisms: impact (employees see how they have an effect on the customer), appreciation (employees feel valued by the end user), and empathy (employees feel more connected and committed to helping another human being). One example shared found that introducing the end user to a group of call center employees led to increases of more than 400 percent in average weekly revenue! Sharing feedback on the customer experience is a terrific way to build emotional connections for employees. Letting them either hear (listen in on calls) or review customer commentary is an overlooked opportunity in most companies. Sharing successes learned and challenges to be focused on not only makes good business sense, it's an opportunity to REMIND employees about

the branded experience they are responsible for delivering. And, it's another way for managers to demonstrate that they are Managing the Experience.

4. **ENGAGED Customers:** An ENGAGED customer is a loyal customer. They appreciate that you've taken the opportunity to reach out to them, learn from their experience, and most importantly, act on what they've shared. They will like you for following up the first time, and they will love you when you follow up in the future to share how you've used their feedback to improve the experience your company delivers. An ENGAGED customer helps you by buying more of your stuff more often and telling others they should do the same.

TWO APPROACHES TO A CUSTOMER ENGAGEMENT PROGRAM

When it comes to design, there are two primary approaches to a Customer Engagement Program: Overall Experience and Transactional Experience. The type of approach you use (and how often you run the program) should be determined by your chosen goals and objectives. An Overall Experience approach is ideal if you are looking to get customers' perspectives on multiple points of interaction. The primary objective is to connect with customers to get their input on . . . you guessed it . . . the overall experience doing business with your company and its products or services. On the other hand, if you're looking to find out about the experience customers are having at specific points of interaction, a Transactional approach would be more appropriate. The Transactional approach zeros in on one point of interaction and is designed to collect information from a specific transaction for tactical decisions and instant customer follow-up. This approach should occur right after the transaction is complete so customers can provide accurate feedback. You can determine which type of program works best based on your company's needs. Either way, both the Overall Experience and Transactional Experience approaches lead to Quality Conversations and the opportunity to Fix, Share, and Ring. And both position you to ask "What Else? Who Else?"

An Overall Experience Program

This approach is typically administered a few times per year for a company or any given department. Your company will need the time in between to follow up with the necessary conversations that will enable you to Fix, Share, and Ring. The Overall Experience approach enables you to gather interesting data on how loyal your customers are. I recommend using the Customer Loyalty Index (CLI) as the main portion of your survey design. Using CLI enables you to glean data about loyalty, word of mouth, and overall perceptions of performance. The first four questions are standard for CLI measurement and provide the ammunition for having Quality Conversations (see box on the following page).

In addition, you have the option to ask a few additional questions to better understand:

1. Overall perception: the brand image formed in the customers' minds based on the experience they have with your company
2. Competitive environment: customers' perceptions about competitive choices they have
3. Behavior consistency: customers' perceptions on how consistently employees perform specific behaviors during interactions

4. Strength of business relationship (current vs. desired): determine whether the customers see your company as a vendor or a partner in their success (for business-to-business situations)

Customer Loyalty Index

(Customers rate to indicate levels of satisfaction and loyalty.)

1. Satisfaction with overall performance

Customers are asked to rate whether their expectations were met during a specific or set of interactions.

2. Likelihood to continue buying

Customers are asked to rate how likely it is that they will continue doing business with your company based on their past experience over a specific time period. Even if customers rate their likelihood to continue buying high, that may not always mean they are highly satisfied. Customers may continue doing business with your company even if they are not satisfied because it may be too costly to switch (e.g., costs of breaking existing contracts, replacing technological infrastructure, or having to restructure operations).

3. Likelihood to choose again (as if for the first time)

Customers are asked to rate whether they would choose your company if they had to make the decision again for the first time. This question attempts to measure if customers would continue doing business with your company as if moving to a competitor would incur no costs at all.

4. Likelihood to recommend to others

Customers are asked to rate how likely it is that they would recommend your company to friends or colleagues. Customers who rate this high are the most committed to your company, tend to promote you through positive word of mouth, and are less likely to switch to a competitor even if they encounter service disruptions, errors, product defects, or higher prices. In other words, they are more forgiving if you mess up.

Using a zero-to-ten scale, CLI is calculated as a straight average of responses.

I typically recommend picking a few statements that directly coincide with a few of the Do It indicators from the Living the Brand Assessment (your Company-wide Basic Behaviors). That way, you can captivate the workforce with a gap analysis between the employee perspective and the customer reality. For instance, if you ask the workforce to rate how consistently others that they work with engage in friendly conversation with customers to personalize the experience, then you could ask customers to rate how consistently they receive a friendly and welcoming experience.

A good formula to use when customizing questions is CLI + 3. Why limit it to plus three? Because if you do not set a limit, it will only lead to survey creep[1] that will increase the length of the survey and how long it takes your customers to complete it. Longer surveys annoy customers and won't necessarily give you any more valuable information than you would be able to get in follow-up Quality Conversations.

Using the CLI method helps managers to collect information in ways that make insights easier to understand and act on. It's simple to execute and helps you understand how loyal your customers are, confidently make strategic decisions that improve customer relationships, and start Quality Conversations with customers.

Let's explore an example. Assume you are a manager at a professional services company. You recently surveyed the end-user of your product within a company (let's call him Matt). Here's a graph of the results (super-high satisfaction,

---

1. Survey creep: allowing others to add questions that serve their own agenda, yet tend to diminish the overall customer experience, lower participation, and increase the abandonment rate.

highly likely to recommend, fairly likely to choose again, but low likelihood of continuing to buy).

CUSTOMER LOYALTY INDEX (CLI) EXAMPLE

Taken together, the indicators begin to present a story worthy of a Quality Conversation.

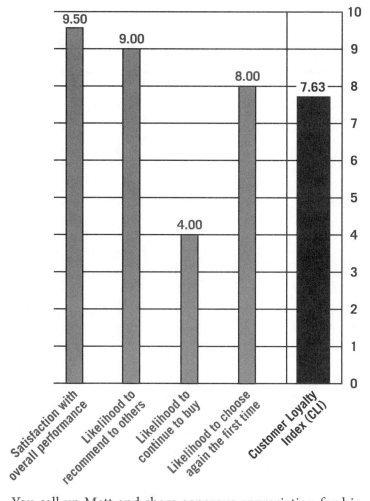

You call up Matt and share generous appreciation for his feedback about his experience doing business with your company. As the conversation begins, you take it down the pathway of inquiring about his survey ratings. You ask why he rated his likelihood to continue to buy so low while rating everything else so high. Matt shares that while he and his colleagues are happy with the product and find that they are up to 20 percent more efficient using it, the CEO is frustrated with the invoicing terms and thinks the company is spending too much. So Matt is being asked to look for other vendors.

Next you call up the CEO and start a conversation with her (let's call her Sarah). You let Sarah know that her people are happy with the products and services your company is providing and note specific aspects that Matt mentioned in your discussion, including the substantial increase in efficiency. Then you share that you understand she is not happy with the invoicing terms and inquire if she would be willing to talk about it. Sarah agrees and after a bit of conversation, you come to agreement on new terms that work for you both.

In this scenario, having the follow-up conversation with Matt (the end user) could result in him referring your company to a few others in his network. At the same time, you had a conversation with the decision maker (Sarah) to fix an issue and rescue the account. In many instances like this, you will also find that the relationship with the decision maker is improved. It is much more likely now that Sarah would be willing to refer your company in the future.

The CLI rating drives the discussion. **Within ten seconds of reviewing the feedback from your short survey, you will know exactly how to start a Quality Conversation**. From there, you can spark a healthy dialogue that gives you plenty to chat about. As well, you will see doors open for referrals, new business, and repeat business. And, you'll also have a more happy and ENGAGED customer.

A Transactional Experience Program

In the Transactional Experience approach, the primary objective is to connect with customers to seek their level of satisfaction at specific experience touchpoints (sales, account management, customer service, technical support, billing, pricing, etc.) during a single transaction (new purchase, annual account meeting, customer service call, etc.). With the Transactional approach, follow-up conversations are focused on connecting with customers to resolve issues, mitigate the impact of unsatisfied customers, and seek out opportunities for a referral (or plant a seed for a future referral). In this approach, you will want to create a list of the key drivers of satisfaction for customers to rate. Think about what is most important to your customer at the specific touchpoint. For instance, if looking to measure satisfaction with account management, then some key indicators of satisfaction would include timeliness, expertise, clarity of communications, and integrity of relationship. Since a Transactional approach is very specific, the instrument used tends to be very short and to the point. As with an Overall Experience approach, your goal is to collect a little meaningful data without overwhelming or intruding on your customer—just enough to spark a Quality Conversation. The following Case In Point shows how a consulting company used the Transactional Experience approach. In this example, you will see the positive impact of asking, "What Else? Who Else?"

Case In Point

Who?

A consulting firm who twenty-four months earlier rolled out a new service and desired client feedback

What's the challenge?

- Faced with two years of flat revenue growth and increasing costs
- Many happy clients, yet very few referrals being provided
- Unsure of true client perspective about new consulting solution

What did they do?

- Built and prioritized list of top 100 decision makers and influencers within fifteen clients using the new solution
- Designed a three-minute survey for initial feedback and input for conducting Quality Conversations with clients
- Conducted follow-up conversations with respondents to discuss the client experience and stimulate "What Else?" (sales) "Who Else?" (referrals) opportunities

What was the result?

- Achieved 59% response rate
- Conducted follow-up Quality Conversations with 72% of respondents in four months
- Over 75% of calls resulted in either a referral or cross-sell/up-sell opportunity

---

DESIGN A PROGRAM THAT DRIVES SALES

Like I've said, investing in a Customer Engagement Program requires an up-front financial investment and people time to design and sustain. But the resulting ROI is well worth it. An initial program design includes, at a minimum, the following components. For each component, I've provided some thought-starters for what to consider. A complete design may go into more depth depending on the complexity of your company, industry, and customer base. From my experience, these steps are the basics. Don't skip any of them. If you do, you risk having a program that won't drive the results that you're looking for.

CUSTOMER ENGAGEMENT PROGRAM DESIGN STEPS

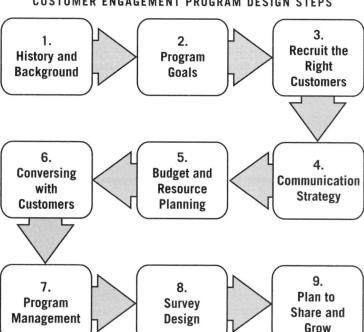

1. **History and Background:** An audit of sorts on the different ways customer feedback has been collected in the past, what was learned, and how the learning was used. This step will help you to uncover what has worked well and not so well and apply the knowledge to guide the upcoming design effort.

2. **Program Goals:** What is it that you are most interested in achieving? Increasing referrals, creating up-selling opportunities, moving stalled accounts, learning about the customer experience and ways to improve it, increasing alignment among managers, further engaging employees, and rescuing potentially lost customers are among the many directions you can choose for program goals.

3. **Recruit the Right Customers:** This step is for determining your segmentation strategy and who to target for feedback on their experience. When segmenting customers, determine what will be most important: years of service, total revenue, industry, geographic location, types of products or services purchased, etc. At this point, you should also make decisions about sample size, reasonable response rates, and frequency of reaching out to gather feedback on the experience.

4. **Communication Strategy:** What will be the most effective ways to invite chosen customers to participate in your Customer Engagement Program? Once decided, a few critical communications include the invite with key messaging, a thank-you for providing feedback, and follow-up communications to start Quality Conversations with customers.

5. **Budget and Resource Planning:** Ensuring follow-up conversations are strategic and effective takes planning, script development, and training. The financial rewards for doing this well far exceed the costs. Budgets and resource planning should be in place long before the launch of the program. You should know who is doing the follow-up emailing, calling, and/or visiting with customers, have all the necessary messaging and scripts, and provide enough initial role-play training so those following up have confidence engaging in relationship-building conversations with customers.

6. **Conversing with Customers:** Having the conversation is critical to learning, building relationships, and growing revenue. *This is the most challenging step in the design of a program.* The quality of the conversations with customers is what drives revenue and profits. It is important to create scripts for those conducting follow-up calls with

customers and develop rules/guidelines so trained employees (the follow-up callers) know how to handle various customer scenarios. A few of the important questions to address include:

- Which customers should receive a follow-up visit versus a phone call or an email?
- Who should conduct the follow-up conversations? Frontline employees? Frontline managers? Account managers? Executives? A specially trained task force?
- When will the follow-up be most effective?
- What happens after the follow-up is complete?

Note: A case management software program such as Salesforce.com, Zendesk.com, or Microsoft Dynamics should be considered for effective tracking of conversations, follow-up guidelines, compliance, and reporting on results such as add-on sales, problems resolved, or learning of an employee-driven success that a customer shared. Software programs like these provide the necessary "trigger" alerts that notify managers and those responsible for follow-up conversations about the opportunity to respond to a customer's feedback.

7. **Program Management:** Who will own the responsibility for keeping the company focused on customer engagement and loyalty? The chosen managers will be responsible for running the program, acting on the information, and driving accountability across the company to collect, converse, share results, and drive improvements and sales. Typically, program management consists of three levels:

- An Executive Sponsor responsible for aiding the program's visibility and viability. This individual should demonstrate a passion for customer centricity and display strong communication throughout the company. While this person is not involved in the day-to-day, it is critical that he or she meets with the rest of the team at regular intervals.

- Business Function Owners responsible for driving improvement across their business functions, departments, or work areas. This group sets goals and reviews performance regularly. Typical functions include Sales, Marketing, Operations, IT, Support, Account Management, and Product and Solutions.

- A Program Team that runs the infrastructure behind the program, provides education, prepares analysis, and distributes information to internal functions/departments so they can improve engagement and create more loyal customers who refer your company. These individuals should be expected to be the most knowledgeable resources about the effort within the company and remain up to speed on best practices and lessons learned. In many instances, the Program Team is one internal person who partners with an outside third-party vendor.

8. **Survey Design:** Survey design is the step of building your questionnaire. With the Transactional approach, this is the step for determining the key satisfaction drivers based on what is most important to customers at the specific touchpoint. For an Overall Experience approach, remember the formula CLI + 3. Choose your additional questions wisely based on what will lead to the best data to act on and greatest opportunity to connect with customers during follow-up conversations that strengthen relationships and grow sales. Designing your survey can get very emotional, especially if there are several different business units involved who interact with the customer as each may bring his or

her own agenda about what would be interesting to learn. Protect against survey creep. When considering adding additional questions to the survey, ask your team, "Can we make a decision or take action based on the answer to this question?" and, "Can we more effectively get responses to this question in a follow-up conversation with the customer?" Immediately eliminate the nice-to-know questions whose responses you cannot act on. Companies that are most successful with a Customer Engagement Program do not allow more than ten questions or allow the survey to take more than three minutes to complete.

9. **Plan to Share and Grow:** This is the step where you determine how to share the customer feedback you receive with the workforce. Draft a plan for sharing results to REMIND the workforce about the power of the branded experience and reinforce their "on stage" performance. This is also the time to determine how customer feedback fits into your Living the Brand System. Compare your Customer Loyalty Index to your Employee ENGAGED Index to show strength of relationship. Go further and incorporate feedback from customers into hiring, onboarding, performance reviews, or leadership development systems.

TURN EVERYDAY CUSTOMERS INTO MORE PROFITABLE, ENGAGED CUSTOMERS

Let's face it. Getting feedback from customers really is a selfish act, and that's perfectly okay! Just accept the fact that you want feedback because you want your customers to like you more, buy more from you, and recommend you to friends, relatives, and colleagues. You want to learn and improve so you can outbehave your competition. It goes without saying—happy or satisfied customers will reward your company with long-term loyalty, more business, and referrals. A Customer Engagement Program is the most effective way to start Quality Conversations with your customers that will strengthen relationships and enable you to learn about the experience they receive.

Every time you have the opportunity to interact with customers and learn about their experience, you stimulate potential referrals and up-selling opportunities. But as you've learned, **there is much more to it than simply getting the survey out. Getting the survey out is the easy part. Any monkey can do it. Asking the right questions and following up in an effective manner with Quality Conversations that drive results is what it takes to turn everyday customers into more profitable, ENGAGED customers.**

COMPARING EMPLOYEE AND CUSTOMER EXPERIENCE: A 360° VIEW OF YOUR COMPANY EXPERIENCE

Before we move on, let's circle back to the Metrics That Matter Most.

LIVING THE BRAND SYSTEM

A Customer Engagement Program is one more piece of your Living the Brand System that will help you QUANTIFY your efforts to deliver a branded experience.

Combining customer insights and data with the insights and data from

140

your Living the Brand Assessment are two pieces that feed into a 360° View of your branded experience—helping to paint the picture of how the employee work culture and customer experience are helping to improve financial results. Consider the benefits of comparing your com-

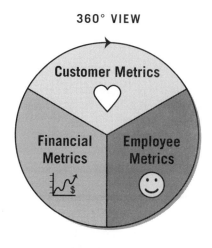

360° VIEW

pany's Employee ENGAGED Index to customer satisfaction and loyalty metrics. Think about how valuable it would be to show how improving the consistency of one Company-wide Basic or Job-specific Behavior in a department could lead to measurable improvements in how loyal your customers are.

For managers, this combination will become the most comprehensive way to evaluate the "on stage" performance of their people. In addition, it is a powerful communication opportunity with employees that clearly shows their impact on the customer experience and the financial outcomes your company is striving to reach.

What should you hold your customer experience accountable for?

Metrics That Matter Most

Which metrics should you hold the experience accountable for?

Revenue Generating
1. Repeat business per customer
2. Average sale per customer
3. Profit margin
4. Customer retention
5. Number of referrals
6. Average sale per top 20% of customers
7. Cross-selling/up-selling
8. Hours billed (utilization)
9. Inventory turns
10. Billing cycles
11. Conversion rates

Other: _____
_____
_____

Cost-Reducing
1. Employee turnover
2. Unwanted employee turnover
3. Quality issues
4. Product returns
5. Employee absenteeism
6. Legal expense
7. Marketing expense
8. Training expense
9. Safety issues
10. Time to fill a job
11. Employee theft

Other: _____
_____
_____

POWER OF THE PAUSE

- Is your company currently annoying customers with lengthy satisfaction surveys?
- Who in your company would be ideal for conducting Quality Conversations with customers to strengthen relationships and grow sales?
- How many "What Else? Who Else?" conversations would you like to see happen in your company each week?

Put the Carrots Away, Rewards Don't Work the Way You Think They Do

---

HIGHLIGHTS

1. A strategic recognition program that facilitates the capturing and sharing of successes and best practices on a daily basis is a great way to replicate what your best employees are doing. Unfortunately, a gap exists between what research has proven in regard to the science of recognition and what managers actually do when implementing recognition/reward programs. Most programs fail because of low participation, too much focus on rewards, too little focus on driving business results, and lack of leadership buy-in to recognition as a strategic management discipline.

2. The reality is, we've been conditioned to think of rewards and recognition as a pair that must go together when, in fact, quite often they don't. Employees get much greater value from the power of recognition and much less from the actual rewards. Therefore, the two do not need to go together to be optimally effective.

3. Managers who master the skill set of genuinely and proactively recognizing people are able to most effectively REMIND employees of what it takes to Live the Brand.

MAKE A WISH

Imagine a genie showed up at your next quarterly financial review meeting and granted your management team one wish. But, as is usually the case with genies, there's a catch . . . you can only wish for one of two outcomes:

- Outcome 1: A healthier, faster-growing economy. With this wish, you have the power to put our economy on a trajectory of strong growth. Your industry grows and you and your competition all have the opportunity to benefit from it.
- Outcome 2: The ability to replicate the experiences delivered by your best employees. With this wish, you can capture the mindset your best employees have about the branded experience, how they act in regard to delivering it, and how they interact with others when performing the experience for customers.

So, what would your management team wish for?

I've been posing this question to audiences of managers for a few years now. During the "Great Recession," responses were interesting. Before really thinking it through, many would quickly wish for the healthier economy, thinking that it would take away some short-term revenue growth challenges. After a bit more thought, these leaders would overwhelmingly agree that if you could replicate what your best employees are doing you would certainly be able to outbehave the competition.

Over time, the economy will take care of itself. And, your competition is competing under the same economic conditions you are. The ability to replicate what your best people do and the experiences they deliver when they are at the top of their game—now that's a competitive differentiator.

If you are trying to build and manage an experience that ENGAGES employees and customers then the choice is easy.

MANAGE AND MEASURE THROUGH STRATEGIC RECOGNITION

Remember: 1 percent of your company's success in Managing and Measuring the Experience will come from documenting and training it. Ninety-nine percent of your success will come from the daily, weekly, and monthly reminders that are put in place and acted upon.

The Living the Brand Assessment and Customer Engagement Program introduced in Principles 5 and 6 are two powerful ways to REMIND others about and QUANTIFY the branded experience—two important pieces of a Living the Brand System. Another way to reinforce what success looks like and make the branded experience part of day-to-day conversations is a Living the Brand Strategic Recognition Program.

LIVING THE BRAND SYSTEM

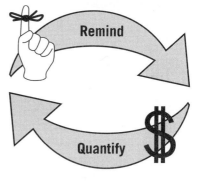

A strategic recognition program that facilitates the capturing and sharing of successes and best practices on a daily basis is a great way to replicate what your best employees are doing. And you'll find it to far surpass any reward-oriented program when it comes to creating ENGAGED employees. So what exactly is a strategic recognition program? And how is it different from a rewards program?

Strategic recognition is the act of acknowledging, appreciating, and sharing a success that helped improve the employee or customer experience— a success that is easily tied to key performance indicators that are already being measured by your company (like customer retention, revenue growth, increased productivity, enhanced brand image, etc.). Let's quickly revisit the 360° View and metrics that matter most. Which important metrics would be most impacted by managers and employees capturing and sharing examples of the experience in action that others can learn from and replicate? (Reference the Metrics That Matter Most chart on the following page.)

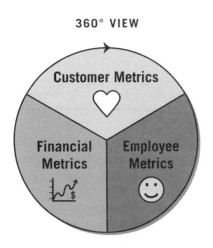

360° VIEW

A Living the Brand Strategic Recognition Program is usually an online or mobile device–based program where employees submit stories (captured successes) of others that they work with delivering the branded experience, going above and beyond, or demonstrating a best practice. The captured successes are then reviewed by managers and posted for all employees to see on a homepage dashboard that also houses program statistics and communication features that have become common practice in a world filled with social media outlets like Facebook and Twitter.

Metrics That Matter Most

Which metrics should you hold the experience accountable for?

Revenue Generating
1. Repeat business per customer
2. Average sale per customer
3. Profit margin
4. Customer retention
5. Number of referrals
6. Average sale per top 20% of customers
7. Cross-selling/up-selling
8. Hours billed (utilization)
9. Inventory turns
10. Billing cycles
11. Conversion rates

Other: _____
_____
_____

Cost-Reducing
1. Employee turnover
2. Unwanted employee turnover
3. Quality issues
4. Product returns
5. Employee absenteeism
6. Legal expense
7. Marketing expense
8. Training expense
9. Safety issues
10. Time to fill a job
11. Employee theft

Other: _____
_____
_____

 Managers who are willing to develop their skills in recognizing others have a great opportunity to leverage it as an effective way to Manage the Experience and REMIND employees to Live the Brand (KNOW the branded experience and DO it consistently). It provides continuous fodder for starting conversations (formally or informally) with your people. And it provides a platform for publicly and privately acknowledging employee actions that led to tangible benefits for your company—linking employee behavior to results to help employees see how they make a difference (which

147

makes them feel good and become more productive and ENGAGED). And participation numbers are another great indicator of the 360° View of results to hold the experience accountable for.

As we dive into this chapter, I must let you know that we are embarking on an area that I have incredible passion for and incredible frustration with more than anything else. That is, the recognition and rewards programs that are supposed to motivate a more ENGAGED and productive workforce. I feel passion because the act of capturing and sharing success not only powers a positive branded experience, it's also the right thing to do. What's frustrating is that I continue to witness such

> **Appreciation is the strongest currency in your corporate culture.**

an egregious and erroneous investment of resources in lame, nonstrategic, and unsustainable rewards programs that produce little or nothing to show in the form of increased engagement, participation, and—most importantly—positive impact on revenue growth and profitability.

It's ridiculous the way many managers think about and act with respect to motivating people. Even given the enormity of research and scientific proof, there still exists a chasm between what research has proven decade after decade and what business leaders actually do. I call this the **Strategic Recognition Chasm,** and it should (and can) be closed. Too many managers have a carrot-and-stick mentality and operate from assumptions about performance that are outdated, not challenged enough, and simply untrue. It's time to put the carrots away!

PUT THE CARROTS AWAY; USE WHAT REALLY MOTIVATES PEOPLE AT WORK

Going back to the 1940s, studies have shown that what motivates people most at work includes understanding how they make a difference and feeling recognized and appreciated for doing a good job. If you throw "relationship with my boss" into the mix, you also have what are typically the top three reasons why someone is loyal to his or her employer. Yet there still exists a Strategic Recognition Chasm between what research has proven and what business leaders and HR professionals do when it comes to investing in and facilitating recognition (not rewards) in the workplace.

> " The reality of employee recognition in the workplace is that much more is needed. Period. "

A study done by the Society of Human Resource Management and Globoforce reported:

- 54 percent of HR leaders do not think managers and supervisors at their company effectively acknowledge and appreciate employees
- 69 percent of HR leaders believe employees are not satisfied with the level of recognition they receive at work
- 32 percent of CEOs invest no time in (and may not even be aware of) their company's employee recognition programs

This seems odd to me for a couple reasons. First, it is common sense that if you want to see more of something from someone then you should use positive reinforcement (appreciation and recognition) when it happens. Well-known

149

and respected author, speaker, and management guru Tom Peters has been saying for years, "Celebrate what you want to see more of." Second, it's not like managers are bad at giving praise. Think about how well most of them acknowledge small achievements regularly with their kids, nephews, nieces, grandkids, etc. Unfortunately it seems as if some managers' ability to see and enthusiastically recognize small improvements wanes over time until one day it takes a major achievement to raise awareness. Too many managers ration out praise as if there will be a shortage of it. And some (as the research indicates) just simply don't believe in—or just don't understand—the power of recognizing effort and results together. How else can you explain how nearly one-third of CEOs invest no time or are completely unaware of the existence of their company's recognition program?

Here's an example from a recent discussion I had with a client. I was meeting with a group of executives from a financial services firm when one of them spoke up and said, "Just last week, Suraj brought to my attention the opportunity to approach an existing client with one of our service offerings that they have never purchased before—an offering that would clearly be of great value. Now why would I need to publicly recognize Suraj for this? He knows that this is something we expect him to do." In this case, Mr. Executive simply wasn't getting it. So I replied, "Would you like to see more people in your company do what Suraj did? Do you want other employees to create cross-selling experiences for your company and experiences for your clients that help them buy more of your offerings? Of course you do. So stop thinking about your company's recognition program as a 'thank-you' program and start thinking about it as a program to capture and share the best practices and experiences that enable positive growth. Sure, Suraj may not need or want the pat on the back (although he probably does) but don't let that stop you from showing that his efforts are appreciated. And most importantly, don't miss the opportunity to allow others in your company to learn from the actions he took to help grow revenue."

Even though you and many of your colleagues know the power of recognition in the workplace, it is not uncommon for managers to forget to do it as often as necessary.

A simple Google search will provide mounting evidence going back seven decades attesting that rewards and incentive schemes rarely work and actually do more harm than good. Yet, companies spend more than $46 billion per year on employee rewards programs, and most managers still rely on bonuses, plaques, motivational posters, and other shiny trophy-like "carrots" to drive employee, and ultimately company, performance.

The Strategic Recognition Chasm drives me crazy. Why? Because it's illogical. Companies are tricked by vendors in the rewards industry into implementing half-baked programs that do not hit the drivers of motivation. These vendors go as far as marketing their rewards programs as employee performance drivers and—get this—culture changing programs! These traditional rewards programs include service or tenure awards, bonuses, and prizes or gifts for hitting business targets (financial, quality, process improvement, etc.). These programs typically have such low

> **Rewards programs don't drive sustainable culture change or business results.**

participation (most I've seen range from 10 to 20 percent regular participation), how could they possibly have an impactful and positive effect on the workforce? The *Journal of Compensation and Benefits* found that fewer than 40 percent of HR managers believe their rewards programs drive measurable impact on employee engagement. Their research also showed that rewards programs are not viewed as initiatives that build and transform culture. Not a surprise! Do you see why this drives me a bit crazy?

Plain and simple: rewards-focused programs don't work to drive financial results the way many leaders think they do. We've been conditioned to think of rewards and recognition as a pair that must go together when, in fact, quite often they don't. I am not suggesting you should recognize and forget about the reward. I am simply suggesting that your company will get much greater value out of the power of recognition and much less from the actual rewards, and that the two don't need to go together to be optimally effective.

Recently I met Alex, an HR manager at a large corporation. She was in the process of scouting out different rewards vendors to implement a "recognition" program within her company and she wanted my advice. Alex mentioned that they recently went through a branding program and updated their corporate values and they wanted a program that would enable real culture change. Alex shared some of the content the rewards vendors provided about the impact their programs have on stock price and employee satisfaction. I wasn't shocked—having seen similar marketing case studies many times before—but I was definitely not a believer. Here is the thinking I shared with Alex: If your rewards vendor claims ROI based on employee satisfaction and shareholder value, you need to question how much of an impact that program is having. In addition, two of the questions you should ask yourself about the rewards vendor are "What is their core competency?" and "How do they make money?" More times than not you will find that the rewards vendor generates 90 percent or more of their revenue from . . . you guessed it . . . rewards.

If Alex is looking for a recognition program to truly drive culture change then she must realize that rewards are only a small part of the equation (if necessary at all), and that participation is critical—especially participation of management. If the great majority of employees are actively participating, then you can make ROI claims like the ones Alex shared with me. However, that's rarely, if ever, the case. If you design a strategic recognition program that has high participation (by high participation, I mean at least 60 to 75 percent *regular* participation from employees and 90 percent or more *regular* participation from management—not "one and done" participation) then you can create real ROI examples. You can show trends that indicate evidence of strength of relationship between participation and the financial measures you care most about. A typical rewards company can never make those claims because their weekly, monthly, and annual participation rates are not high enough, no matter what the type of carrot they dangle for rewards. They are more focused on selling rewards to the few than making behavior change happen for the many.

I've seen too many examples of good companies who have succumbed to the misconception of rewards as motivators for performance. For example, Brand Integrity was invited to meet with executives of a publicly held company frustrated with the lack of return on its $1.2 million annual spending on rewards. What we found was a significant divide among HR executives who were defending their budget and business line leaders who were finding that the rewards were not driving any sustainable behavior change and had only limited business results. To make matters worse, within six months they had already eaten up close to 75 percent of their allocated budget for the year. Does this sound familiar?

How about the story of a global airline spending $45 million annually in rewards and bonuses to improve customer results? Would it surprise you that a senior leader said that while it felt good to dole out $45 million to reward employees, he wasn't sure the company had achieved a meaningful system that could truly drive behavior change? How do you think customers and shareholders would feel about this?

 These companies are not alone. In fact, many of you reading this are probably guilty of falling for—or have been asked to participate in—a similar type of "carrots"-focused approach. If your company's rewards program seems like a "flavor-of-the-month" activity or isn't having the impact on employee engagement and productivity that you think it should, it's time to consider something else. Let's look at a fundamentally different approach, based on research into the science of motivation, which shows a clear link to business results and doesn't require any investment in rewards.

DESIGNING A LIVING THE BRAND STRATEGIC RECOGNITION PROGRAM

 Today we have much improved communication tools and techniques to help facilitate recognition to create powerful reminders of the branded experience. Web-based and mobile software platforms make it simple to facilitate, manage, and measure employee recognition, enabling your managers to Manage the Experience while fueling the strong desire of employees to be appreciated and recognized. Strategic recognition efforts should power a company attitude and effort to Live the Brand and support any and all efforts to ENGAGE the workforce with your branded experience. Measuring recognition activity adds a level of superior visibility and accountability for all employees and is ultimately how behavior change happens. Behavior change is what takes your company from culture talk to real culture change. And again, no "carrots" needed.

A well-designed strategic program not only provides powerful reminders, but also helps meet the growing need for immediate and consistent feedback at work. When done well, recognition enables managers to do three responsibilities extremely well:

1. **Set expectations.** By fostering an environment of capturing and sharing successes and best practices, managers are able to reinforce the expectation of what it takes to KNOW and DO the branded experience (Live the Brand).

2. **Strategically communicate.** Managers are equipped with a weekly, if not daily, way to converse about examples of successes, best practices, and Living the Brand Moments.[1] Managers can share these examples at daily "huddle" meetings, weekly staff meetings, and in day-to-day dialogue. Making the branded experience a part of the conversation

---

1. Living the Brand Moment: a captured success that is an example of someone performing the branded experience in a way that has or will have a clear impact on cost reduction, productivity, or profitability.

is critical to keeping the workforce ENGAGED with the idea that they are on stage delivering an experience for each other and customers.

3. **Hold themselves and others accountable.** When capturing and sharing successes is an expected practice, leaders are able to collect data on participation by region, department, team, or all the way down to the individual contributor level. This visibility into who is Living the Brand and who is seeing it (recognizing it) establishes an unheard of level of accountability. This accountability is achieved when recognition is used to serve up daily reminders and spark meaningful conversations.

The complexity of the program depends on the company; one size does not fit all. The following are the top critical-to-success components to designing a Living the Brand Strategic Recognition Program that is sustainable and profitable. You can review each component and determine which will be most valuable for your department or company.

A Living the Brand Strategic Recognition Program should . . .

1. Engage everyone
2. Connect successes to business outcomes
3. Be accessible to drive high participation
4. Fuel a reminding engine
5. Use points and badges to make it "sticky"
6. Make the most impactful successes shine
7. Feed the social appetite
8. Spark meaningful conversations
9. Enable managers to measure and manage results

Let's take a closer look at each component.

1. **Engage everyone**

   True or false: Everyone in a company is responsible for Living the Brand and can recognize when others are living it. True! This should be your mode of thinking. Don't tolerate rewards programs that generate limited participation. All employees should be responsible to participate by being a witness of the branded experience in one of two ways:

   - Peer-to-peer captured success: the act of KNOWING what an on-brand experience looks like, witnessing an individual or a small group (yes, your program should allow the capturing of group successes) DOING an on-brand experience, and capturing it in the program. This includes capturing successes from employee to employee as well as from employee to manager and manager to employee.

   - Personal best practice: the act of capturing a best practice you've done or idea that you have that would be beneficial to share with others. This is ideal for remote employees who don't have as much visibility or are not as visible to others in their day-to-day work.

   In both of these cases, successes and Living the Brand Moments are captured and shared so that others can learn and employees receive acknowledgment. If the expectation is that everyone participates, before you know it you'll have woven the act of witnessing and capturing the success of others into the corporate culture, helping to replicate the thinking and actions that some employees rarely do or only do on their best days.

   The following Case In Point is an example of how strategic recognition can enhance customer retention and desired financial outcomes.

Case In Point

Who?

Nationwide distributor of commercial and residential equipment

What's the challenge?

- Numerous challenges facing the business: change in leadership, lack of alignment across geographic locations, transition from public to private, and negative selling from competition
- Desire to improve the employee and customer experience and get the entire company focused on one goal
- Lack of formal recognition or feedback channel to manage the experience and culture transformation
- Lack of formal team dedicated to leading culture change efforts

What did they do?

- Clearly defined the branded experience (Company Mindset and Company-wide Basic Behaviors everyone can and should do)
- Implemented a strategic recognition program for capturing and sharing successes, best practices, and above and beyond moments
- Made it easy for employees to submit stories and captured successes online, from mobile phones, and through a call center
- Empowered each office and call center to creatively share weekly examples via bulletin boards and TV displays

What was the result?

- $5 million increase in customer retention within the first year
- Among 1,500 employees 4,250 successes were captured and shared within two years
- 82% of the workforce actively participates in the program
- Employees are more focused, empowered, and productive while also creating a customer-centric culture

---

2. **Connect successes to business outcomes**

There is a tremendous opportunity to create a culture focused on Living the Brand simply by modifying the program approach to include both the branded experience and business results. This is not common and in fact, prior to 2006, in an in-depth patent search I could not find one example in the United States of a program where employees were recognized for both demonstrating the branded experience and hitting a business outcome. Even today, only 37 percent of HR leaders say they tie employee recognition programs to corporate values and less than half (43 percent) recognize employees based on performance related to the company's financial goals. This reality alone is why it is so important to think of your recognition efforts as "strategic." Doing so enables you to get employees to see how what they do helps drive company success. And employees sure do want to learn more about how they make a difference, don't they? Every time an employee captures a success, he or she should be focused on business results. It is a learning opportunity for employees to see how their actions and the actions of others translate into results.

To download a strategic recognition form for cap

> Follow the link http://engagedbook.com/recognition to access a tool for capturing and sharing success.

turing successes use the link provided here. You can customize it to meet your unique needs. The components are simple and straightforward. And best of all . . . the form includes a clear link to business outcomes that managers care most about.

See the Case In Point on the following page for an example of strategic recognition driving specific business outcomes.

3. **Be accessible to drive high participation**

Make sure your recognition program is easy to access. To ensure high participation, you've got to get to the workforce where they are, whether that's on their smartphones and tablets or in an offline format. Today more than 50 percent of U.S. mobile phone users are on a smartphone, and the percentage is increasing rapidly. Even if your current

---

Case In Point

Who?

A department within a professional service firm

What's the challenge?

- Employees not effectively cross-selling or up-selling additional services
- Continuously losing sales opportunities because clients are unaware of the variety of services available

What did they do?

- Used strategic recognition program to initiate and track a one-month cross-selling contest for all employees
- Provided employees a simple training on how to initiate cross-selling discussions
- Instructed employees to capture and share examples of cross-selling and up-selling activity every week (regardless of outcome)

What was the result?

- Twenty-four cross-selling opportunities within the first three weeks led to a 500% return on investment
- Strengthened relationships and ongoing sales opportunities with clients by providing additional value
- Changed culture by helping employees see and act on up-selling and cross-selling opportunities

---

 workforce is not on mobile devices, it's plain to see that the trend is moving toward smaller devices like tablets and mobile phones. It's better to plan now! Going mobile is another great way to RE-MIND the workforce about the branded experience—it's literally in the palms of their hands. In addition, make sure to plan alternate avenues for offline employees to capture successes. The goal is ease of access—if your program is cumbersome, employees are less likely to join in. Call-in lines, kiosks, and paper-based forms are a few ways to make it simple for offline employees to participate.

4. **Fuel a reminding engine**

Creating visibility is important to ensure the success of any recognition program. Employees and managers should be able to read daily and weekly newsfeeds from your recognition homepage, dashboard, or from a company intranet site. Sharing great examples of people Living the Brand serve as frequent reminders to keep people using the program and also increase the exposure of best practices and experiences you'd like replicated. In addition, implementing an email alert (similar to a Google Alert) makes it easy for managers to be notified when their direct reports receive recognition or submit a captured success. For companies with a large offline population, engaging employees with printable certificates that can be posted in common areas and offices is another great way to maintain visibility.

Today, companies are highly geographically dispersed with many employees working from home, remotely, or from different offices. As a result, a lot of companies lack opportunities for face-to-face recognition from peers and managers. While technology offers the opportunity to work remotely, it does not diminish the overwhelming desire people have to feel connected and to be appreciated for the work they do. Your recognition program must be designed to keep them in the reminder loop, allowing them to be touched weekly, if not daily, with successes and Living the Brand Moments.

The Case In Point on the following page shows strategic ways to drive participation and desired business results.

Case In Point

Who?

Full service convenience stores

What's the challenge?

- Employees not consistently delivering the core values and many stores falling well below expectations
- Did not want to be seen as a "low cost provider," yet customers indicated low prices as the primary reason for shopping
- Desire to change customer perspective to "employees" and/or the "experience delivered" as a reason for shopping

What did they do?

- Started a Mystery Shopper program to help measure effectiveness of customer interactions
- Clearly defined Job-specific Behaviors for customer service that aligned with Mystery Shopper goals and objectives
- Instituted semi-annual surveys to measure Job-specific Behavior consistency (at store and employee level)
- Provided workforce with coaching and training focused on delivering and measuring the branded experience
- Engaged workforce with strategic recognition program focused on enhancing the work environment and delighting customers

What was the result?

- Achieved 88% employee participation in strategic recognition program in one year
- Averaged 9 above and beyond moments shared per employee and nearly 200 per store in one year
- Behavior consistency increased across all customer service behaviors within one year
- 11% increase in Mystery Shopper scores in two years
- 14% increase in overall customer service scores in two years
- 11% increase in revenue over two years
- $2.21 increase in average sale over two years

5. **Use points and badges to make it "sticky"**

People like to keep score. And when the score is kept, more people pay attention. Especially the younger generation in our workforce as is evidenced by the trend toward gamification in the workplace. In learning about gamification, I've found that in most cases, incorporating it into the culture is beneficial to a company in that it helps keep people focused on performing the branded experience. Gamification typically applies to things we don't like to think of as games. It's often used to help make technology more appealing, thus encouraging users to get more involved, passionately keeping score and tracking success.

One way companies leverage technology and gamification is by introducing points within their Living the Brand Strategic Recognition Program. Here are a few creative ways I've seen points distributed:

- To individuals who see others Living the Brand and capture a success
- To employees who are caught demonstrating the branded experience (the subject of the captured success)
- To every employee with the expectation that on a weekly or monthly basis they are to distribute points to individuals they witness Living the Brand

Points can be associated with a monetary value, and some programs let employees redeem points for gift cards, merchandise from the company store, as a donation to the charity of their choice, or even for a day off to rejuvenate or work on a special project. However, as I stated earlier, recognition and rewards are two different things. Points don't need to have a monetary value and can simply be a fun way to "gamify" the program.

Badges are another gamification technique to drive usage of the program and increase its "stickiness." Badges are a special form of recognition earned at different achievement levels. Using the technique of badges enables a more progress- and milestone-driven type of recognition. Some badges may be earned at easy-to-reach milestones like the "Captured Two Successes in a Month" badge or the "Delighted a Customer" badge. Or badges may be earned at milestones that are more difficult to reach such as the "Was Recognized Ten Times" badge. Badges serve to make the company experience personal; people enjoy checking their progress and the "game" aspect makes it fun.

6. **Make the most impactful successes shine**

   Not all captured successes are of equal value. Some may be a simple thank-you for doing something that in many cases is just doing your job but doing it very well— setting the standard for others—and some may be for going above and beyond the normal job requirements. Living the Brand Moments are truly WOW moments that have a profound impact on cost savings or revenue generation. It's the responsibility of managers to make sure the best ones stand out. When a success is submitted it should go through a managerial approval process. Doing so adds another layer of visibility for managers into the activities their employees do to impact the employee or customer experience. The most successful programs I've witnessed over the better part of the last decade use a three-tiered approach for categorizing captured successes:

   - **One Star:** A thank-you for doing your job. Ideal for situations when you want to reinforce the "right" way of doing something or to provide reinforcement to an employee who may not typically do a specific activity consistently.

- **Two Star:** An act that is considered above and beyond the standard job requirement. A best practice that you wish more people would take the initiative to do.
- **Three Star:** Reserved for WOW moments. Ideal for any action performed by an employee or group of employees that has or will have a clear impact on cost reduction, productivity, or profitability.

Three Star successes become powerful examples that managers can use to REMIND the workforce about the branded experience and its impact on the employee and customer experience. Managers can highlight Three Star successes as examples during one-on-one or team meetings, during the hiring and onboarding processes, in performance conversations, or through special recognition.

7. **Feed the social appetite**

A continuous posting of captured successes is critical, yet it is still not enough to feed recognition-starved employees, especially those with significant social appetites created by Facebook, Twitter, Instagram, Pinterest, and LinkedIn. This is especially true for the Gen Y age group (born between 1981 and 2000) who've grown up in a world of point scoring (gaming) and in families with constant feedback and praise. In the Gen Y world, second place still gets a trophy. In fact, it's not uncommon for everyone who played to get a trophy. Recently a CEO complained to me that, "Every Gen Y we've hired wants feedback at the end of their first day, a trophy at the end of the week, and a pay raise at the end of their first month." While this is clearly an exaggeration (and quite a funny one in my opinion), it does reflect the reality that this generation has views about feedback and acceptable ways of sharing information that are different from prior generations. Not right or wrong, just different. And let's give them some credit for upping the demand for communication and recognition at work. Having a portal for sharing best practices and posting comments will make your program more visible and stimulate higher participation. There are many ways to satisfy the need for socialization in your strategic recognition program:

- Create a constant feed of Living the Brand activity that provides employees the opportunity to comment (in 140 characters or less, of course). Enabling comments on posted successes lets managers further engage employees by showing appreciation and acknowledging the impact of the activity in an informal way. Posting comments in the same manner as an update on Facebook or a "Tweet" gets more people to see it, generating conversations that keep the branded experience top of mind. Recently I received a call from the CEO of a manufacturing company. A few weeks earlier he learned about the capability in his company's strategic recognition program to make comments on nominations. He stated, "This commenting stuff has made me a much better communicator at work. It's really changed my life! I take five minutes a week to review a few captured successes and make a few short comments. Employees love it and they can't believe how passionate I am for living our brand. I'm really having fun with it too." Five minutes a week. That's all it takes.

- Another way to feature the most impactful successes is to include a voting or "liking" functionality (similar to what we've become accustomed to on Facebook and other social media sites). Brand Integrity clients use a feature called

Spotlight for high-impact Living the Brand Moments that indicate a success of particular importance.

- Allow employees to "share" successes they want others to see. Sharing sends another employee or small group of employees a note to view a specific success. It helps to more easily spread best practices across an employee base—ultimately making it easier for others to replicate the experience.

- Set up the program so individuals can capture group successes to encourage and recognize teamwork.

- Establish public Personal Profiles to let employees track their Living the Brand success over time as well as view the success of others.

8. **Spark meaningful conversations**

Every captured success fuels an opportunity to REMIND others about the importance of delivering the branded experience and provides fodder to spark meaningful conversations. One example is the performance review conversation. Brand Integrity has been conducting research over the past five years on a series of behavioral indicators. Every year, the indicator "hold important conversations when needed" is rated at the very bottom. Our informal research is further supported by an SHRM report stating that 44 percent of HR leaders don't feel that employees are rewarded according to job performance. This is because job performance is too subjective if managers do not consistently have healthy conversations about expectations with employees. Designing your program to have a public Personal Profile for each employee enables managers to quickly look up an individual's activity for a given period of time.

Having access to the captured successes or Living the Brand Moments an individual witnessed as well as the examples when he or she was recognized makes it much easier to hold an objective performance conversation. Typically, managers do an annual review and work hard to try and remember anything beyond the last few months. This creates frustration for both the manager and employee. Showing up to a performance review conversation with an employee's self-assessment of how consistently he or she delivers the Company-wide Basic Behaviors and a month-to-month record of captured successes makes for a considerably more meaningful dialogue on what success looks like. In addition, it enables managers to proactively reinforce the behaviors and experiences they want to see more of.

9. **Enable managers to measure and manage results**

Eighty-seven percent of companies do not currently track recognition program ROI, and 68 percent of HR leaders say they find it difficult to measure the effectiveness of their recognition efforts. I can assure you, using the design components I've just outlined can take your program to 100 percent measurable results. Let's look again at the metrics chart to see what you can hold your recognition efforts accountable for (see chart on following page). Quantifying the results helps foster the much needed support and investment from senior leadership who ultimately must continue to fund the program. In every company I've ever worked with, across dozens of industries, the data and focus on results help to close the Strategic Recognition Chasm. Leaders see the value of strategic recognition and—over time—change what they do. When they change what they do, culture changes and the workforce more consistently Lives the Brand.

Metrics That Matter Most

Which metrics should you hold the experience accountable for?

Revenue Generating	Cost-Reducing
1. Repeat business per customer	1. Employee turnover
2. Average sale per customer	2. Unwanted employee turnover
3. Profit margin	3. Quality issues
4. Customer retention	4. Product returns
5. Number of referrals	5. Employee absenteeism
6. Average sale per top 20% of customers	6. Legal expense
7. Cross-selling/up-selling	7. Marketing expense
8. Hours billed (utilization)	8. Training expense
9. Inventory turns	9. Safety issues
10. Billing cycles	10. Time to fill a job
11. Conversion rates	11. Employee theft
Other: _____	Other: _____
_____	_____
_____	_____

Here's an example that shows the thinking necessary to use employee recognition at work in a way that truly ENGAGES employees, creates a stronger Living the Brand culture, and, best of all, enables a company to replicate its best people and the experiences they perform.

Two years ago our sales team met with a health-care provider with 3,500 employees. They had worked with the same rewards vendor for more than a decade, spending north of $240,000 per year buying traditional employee rewards. It was shared with our team that, in previous years, between 10 and 20 percent of their employees would receive awards and that if any more than that were rewarded the budget would simply be too high. The team of leaders seemed discouraged and concerned with the lack of impact the program was having. They were leery of continuing down the same "we've always done it this way" path and were ripe for a new approach that would provide bottom-line results. In winning their business, we knew we needed to help them see the world of recognition a bit differently. Our goal was to help them see the power of recognition in the workplace and diminish their dependence on the reward ("carrot") component. We asked a few questions to get them thinking:

- How are successes captured and shared in your company so others can learn from them?
- Are you rewarding employees for outcomes or the behaviors and experiences delivered to drive those outcomes?
- Is it a concern to you that, in any given year, 80 to 90 percent of your workforce is not recognized within your current program?

Our dialogue opened their minds to a potentially better way. We shared that if they followed our Living the Brand Strategic Recognition Program they would achieve at least 70 percent participation throughout their workforce in the first year. And that this number would grow year after year. We told them if they did not achieve 70 percent they should consider their program a failure! The executives were starting to get excited.

They were even more excited when we said they could repurpose their $240,000 rewards budget to more strategic usage, that is, in ways that would truly drive financial results. That's right—they did not need to invest in any rewards.

Are you curious about the result?

This health-care company embarked on implementing a recognition program that amazed them. In nine short months they achieved 70 percent participation. In just over one year they captured more than 10,000 successes of employees at all levels Living the Brand. And they did this without one penny of rewards.

YOUR LAST STEP ON YOUR JOURNEY TO A MORE ENGAGED WORKFORCE AND MORE ENGAGED CUSTOMERS

Your Living the Brand System enables you to manage the culture (employee experience) and customer experience and quantify them, which in turn raises employee morale and increases their loyalty. It also drives greater loyalty from customers, which helps your company to grow. When most of your employees and customers are loyal you'll know you've reached ENGAGED status!

Keep in mind, your company needs to do three things to implement a Living the Brand System:

1. Clearly DEFINE the behaviors that make for a great work culture and customer experience.

2. REMIND employees about the delivery of

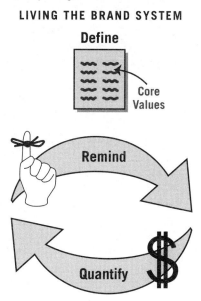

LIVING THE BRAND SYSTEM

Define

Core Values

Remind

Quantify

the experience—clearly setting expectations, communicating, and holding everyone accountable.

3. QUANTIFY the experience and link it to financial metrics.

The first part of this book equipped you with tools for building the beliefs and behaviors that make up your company's branded experience. Principles 5, 6, and 7 outlined the important tools and techniques for measuring the branded experience, communicating about it, and creating a culture of responsibility for living it. The eighth and final Principle presents the concept of managing the branded experience in ways that will help you (and all managers in your company) become a more trusted leader.

POWER OF THE PAUSE

- Are you rewarding employees for outcomes or recognizing them for the behaviors and experiences performed to drive those outcomes?
- What will create the ideal environment where your workforce can become more motivated, productive, and committed to the success of your company: a rewards program or a strategic recognition program?

Manage the Experience to Build Trust in You as a Leader

HIGHLIGHTS

1. Trust is the most important outcome for a leader to achieve. Companies depend on their managers to be good leaders. Without solid leadership people simply won't follow, which leaves the leader with no one behind him or her. You'll earn more trust as a "manager of people" when you learn to effectively and consistently Manage the Experience.

2. If you've defined the branded experience and instituted ways to quantify and measure it yet do nothing with the results, there are going to be predictive consequences with respect to employee frustration, low morale, and a less consistent customer experience. However, if you master some of the basic habits for effectively reminding the workforce, you will not only earn greater trust as a leader, you will end up with a much more ENGAGED workforce around you.

3. Managers earn trust when they make their company's branded experience part of the day-to-day conversation. Making it part of the conversation is a leadership skill to be learned, practiced, and mastered over time. It will become an asset for managers as part of their key role in setting expectations about, communicating about, and holding themselves and others responsible for delivering the branded experience.

THE ECONOMICS OF ENGAGEMENT: SAVE MONEY; MAKE MONEY

Every company wants more ENGAGED employees who consistently deliver the branded experience and more ENGAGED customers who fall in love with you and buy more of your stuff. You want that too or you wouldn't be in the final leg of your journey through the Eight Principles of *ENGAGED!*

As a manager, supervisor, executive, business owner, or whatever you consider yourself, it is your ultimate responsibility to understand what it will take to outbehave the competition. It is your responsibility to create an environment where employees are happy, productive, and ENGAGED—because unhappy employees do not consistently create happy and ENGAGED customers. It is up to you to ensure that the experience is clearly defined as a mindset (beliefs, core values, etc.) and from a behavioral perspective (Company-wide Basic Behaviors, Job-specific Behaviors, Leadership/Managerial Behaviors).

> **Making the branded experience a part of the conversation every day is one of the best ways to build trust and Manage the Experience.**

In order to successfully Manage the Experience, you need to constantly measure and quantify the experience, keeping it visible with strategic reminders that make the experience part of day-to-day conversations. You should be gathering feedback from customers on the experience they're actually having and using it to inform the workforce of the impact they have—reinforcing that employees are on stage delivering an experience that ENGAGES customers, builds relationships, and drives sales. You need to become proficient at capturing examples of when people are Living the Brand and delivering experiences that make your company more successful. And you need to make sure to share those examples as constant reminders of the importance of Living the Brand and to fuel a learning engine to help the workforce replicate the best experiences that ENGAGE customers and make for a great place to work.

If you are not trusted by your peers and employees, it will negatively impact the level of engagement they have in their work. We can agree on that, right? According to John Whitney, author and professor at Columbia Business School, "Mistrust doubles the cost of doing business." Whitney is right on—lack of trust and confidence in leadership does double the cost of doing business. And in some companies that may be an understatement. Let's explore the economics of engagement to get an up close and personal look at the outcomes that are affected.

THE ECONOMICS OF ENGAGEMENT FORMULA

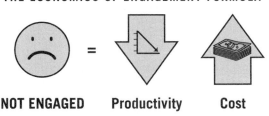

NOT ENGAGED Productivity Cost

Engagement impacts productivity and cost. Productivity is the speed and effectiveness of how work gets done. When employees are not ENGAGED they tend to lack the urgency or desire to go above and beyond or do the necessary actions to protect the quality of products and services. This leads to a less productive environment. And low productivity tends to make it cost a whole lot more to accomplish work as additional financial resources become required. Both of these outcomes negatively impact the customer experience—diminishing your ability to get them ENGAGED.

Do you feel that leaders in your company are in touch with the impacts of engagement? Is there a sense of urgency with respect to further engaging the workforce? Use the link provided to download the Impact of ENGAGED Exercise and find out. It is an exercise you can conduct with a team of managers to get them aligned on the economics of engagement—the reality that high engagement can lead to much better business outcomes while low engagement is very expensive. The exercise helps people discover just how expensive lack of engagement can be.

> ### Low engagement is very expensive!

Follow the link http://engagedbook.com/impactof engaged to access the Impact of ENGAGED Exercise.

ARE YOU A TRUSTED LEADER?

Are you a trusted leader? This question may catch you off guard as it isn't something most managers, supervisors, or executives are often asked, nor is it something most ask themselves.

Take a moment to reflect as it's worth answering: *Do the people you work with trust you as a leader?* I don't mean whether they trust you personally—such as they'd lend you $50 and know you'd pay them back. Nor do I mean whether they trust your competence and character outside of the work environment you operate in—such as would they trust you to perform a tonsillectomy on one of their kids (unless, of course, this happens to be your area of expertise).

If you are like most of the supervisors, managers, and executives I've asked this question to, you are probably not so sure. This can pose problems in driving an ENGAGED workforce that depends on employees trusting their managers, that is, having trust in you.

One of my favorite business quotes (and I'm not so sure where it originated from) is, "People do business with people they like." I first heard this quote as part of a sales training program and quickly realized the relevance to other areas of life—especially leadership. Let's modify this quote just a bit to fit into the context needed here: "People do business with people they like *and trust*." To apply it to leadership, *people* refers to employees you work with, supervise, and manage. To achieve a highly ENGAGED status among employees depends on your ability to earn their trust. It depends on their confidence that you as their manager (and leader) will Live the Brand, not simply try to hold them accountable for living it. Employees need to trust that you understand the branded experience, passionately deliver it each day, and ensure others are doing the same. You'll earn more trust as a "manager of people" when you learn to effectively and consistently Manage the Experience. To do this you need tools. In this chapter I'll share proven tools used by companies who are successful at building trust in management and engaging employees with the branded experience.

There are more books and blogs on leadership than I can count. Having read many of these over the years, it has become evident that the good ones say the same thing just in different ways. Most leadership models tend to pose a common, yet fundamental, role of the leader: to inspire others. Inspiration enables leaders to influence others and have an impact on the way they think and act. And an employee's willingness to be influenced wholeheartedly depends on whether he or she trusts the leader.

Inspiration requires trust! Trust is the most important outcome for a leader to achieve. Without it people simply won't follow, leaving the leader with no one behind him or her. Without trust, why should people do what you (as a leader) ask or suggest? Especially if what you're asking them to do is something that is challenging or simply not in their natural way of doing things. When it comes to creating a culture that is Living the Brand—one that KNOWS the branded experience and DOES it consistently—you can try and demand compliance, but what you really must do is earn adoption and commitment through trust.

BUILD TRUST BY MANAGING THE EXPERIENCE

Your initial journey through *ENGAGED!* is almost done. You've learned how a Living the Brand System enables your company to DEFINE, REMIND others about, and QUANTIFY the branded experience. While successfully implementing a Living the Brand System will get you most of the way there, it is not all there is to it. As a manager, you have to Manage the Experience. If you do nothing with the results you collect from quantifying the experience, there will be predictive consequences. Employees may feel like the Living the Brand System is just another flavor-of-the-month initiative that is doomed to fall to the wayside in a short period of time and so they'll be hesitant to get on board. And it will diminish their trust in you as a leader. The final step to ENGAGED employees (and therefore customers) is to master a few tools and techniques that will make the branded experience part of the day-to-day conversation, creating powerful reminders and helping you make

LIVING THE BRAND SYSTEM

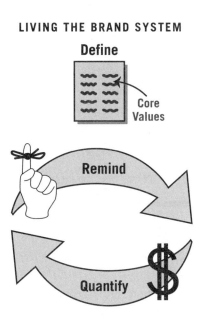

Managing the Experience part of your weekly management practices.

When it comes to soft skills training, remember that the soft stuff really is the hard stuff. It's hard to make it stick. We don't learn important, complex life skills in an instant. In an instant we can get an insight, an "aha," an inspiration. Studies show that only 10 percent of

training is actually implemented. If this is the case, then what percentage of any behavioral or soft skills training is actually retained and practiced (especially if you're not using the right tools)? This is not because of poor content or unproven methodologies for facilitating training. Training events can give us ideas, approaches, checklists, and knowledge. But skills come to us over time through practice and application. To make training "stick" requires consistent reminding and reinforcing.

If you are an executive, you may not see it as your role to be managing the day-to-day. You may feel like the responsibility of Managing the Experience should fall solely on your team of supervisors and managers. Or you may feel like you already have the skill set needed to Manage the Experience, otherwise you wouldn't be where you are today. You may be right, you may be wrong; I'm not here to judge. However, what you can take away from *ENGAGED!* is that your company is counting on you to lead the experience. At a minimum there are three habits you must develop to enable a consistent performance of the branded experience:

1. Live it (don't for a moment think that the nonnegotiable behaviors are for others and not for you).
2. Be aware of the numbers (pay attention to the important numbers and make sure others know them as well—Know It Score, Do It Score, ENGAGED Index, Customer Loyalty Index, strategic recognition program participation, etc.).
3. Make the experience part of the conversation (seek out and act on daily opportunities to mention the experience in group and one-on-one conversations).

MAKING IT PART OF THE CONVERSATION

Making the branded experience a part of the conversation every day is one of the best ways to build trust and Manage the Experience. Learning how is a leadership skill to be studied, practiced, and mastered over time.

When you make the experience part of the conversation, you demonstrate that you know it. Knowing it is the first step toward internalizing it and delivering it consistently. When you KNOW the branded experience and DO it consistently, you start building trust. Making it a part of day-to-day conversation also emphasizes that the branded experience is what defines your company. It REMINDS employees that they are on stage delivering an experience for customers and each other. It's a constant reinforcement of "the way we do things around here."

Think about the number of times every day, week, month, and year that you have the opportunity to REMIND others and ENGAGE them with the branded experience. You may be surprised at how frequently you can spark conversations that help reinforce the importance of Living the Brand. Would you believe me if I told you that you can reach at least 150 reminders per manager a year?

Principles 5, 6, and 7 all introduced ways to REMIND the workforce. The following box contains a recap of those techniques as well as some new techniques and downloadable tools that will help you build trust and Manage the Experience by delivering daily, weekly, and monthly reminders to help the workforce KNOW the branded experience and DO it consistently. These are Essential Habits for any manager, supervisor, or executive (in other words, leader). Let's see how many reminders we can count.

Essential Habits

(Seven key activities and the associated habits that help you to effectively REMIND the workforce by making the branded experience part of the conversation at work.)

1. Ensure an employee assessment, like the Living the Brand Assessment, is done twice a year to measure alignment, engagement, and consistency of delivering the branded experience. **HABIT:** Complete the assessment in a timely manner and encourage participation. That's two reminders.	2
2. Share Living the Brand Assessment results with employees and spark meaningful conversations. **HABIT:** Review strengths, weaknesses, and areas of focus that you and your employees should be accountable for. Two more powerful reminders.	2
3. Gather and integrate feedback from customers. **HABIT:** Seek out input from customers and share it with employees, drawing connections between the work they do and the experience the customer receives. Can you do this one time per month? Great! That's twelve more reminders about the branded experience.	12
4. Implement a program, like the Living the Brand Strategic Recognition Program, for capturing and sharing successes and best practices. **HABIT:** Submit a captured success at least once a month. Another twelve reminders.	12
HABIT: Read notifications of captured successes and share stories in one-on-one and group meetings. If you did this approximately once a week that would be around fifty reminders a year.	50

5. Add the experience to the agenda. **HABIT:** Don't allow a weekly team meeting or shift huddle to start or end without sharing at least one example of someone Living the Brand. Take sixty seconds to focus on an area of the branded experience (specific behavior, a recent success, or a personal goal). Are you part of a weekly meeting? Great! That's approximately fifty more reminder opportunities.	50
6. Hold Necessary Conversations when employees are not delivering the branded experience. **HABIT:** If someone is out of alignment with the branded experience your company wants to deliver, schedule a conversation with him or her that is structured to address performance issues or off-brand behaviors in an objective way focused on setting expectations. Is it reasonable that you have the opportunity to conduct one Necessary Conversation per month? Then let's add twelve more reminders.	12
7. Make decisions using the branded experience. **HABIT:** Use your defined mindset (core values/ brand) when making decisions. Communicate how your decision supports the desired company experience to help increase understanding and buy-in. Can you make ten decisions a year and weave the branded experience into your thinking and justification why? Of course you can. That's ten more, bringing you to 150 possible reminders. And that's just you.	10
Total possible reminders in a year =	**150**

Follow the link http://engagedbook.com/essential habits to access a sample set of tools based on the Essential Habits.

Think about what would happen if every manager in your company could commit to the Essential Habits as great ways to REMIND the workforce to Live the Brand. Just recently, I completed a presentation of these very tools to a group of 135 managers in a large healthcare company. Imagine their surprise when we tallied up the total number of potential reminders for any given year: 20,250 reminders just based on the participants in the room. They were amazed as it became crystal clear to them the profound impact they have in their role. They could clearly see the effect they have on the company culture and customer experience when they do these simple acts to Manage the Experience.

Take a moment and jot down how many managers are in your company that should be responsible for creating (at a minimum) 150 reminders every year. For an example of the power of reminding, see the Case In Point on the following page.

WHAT RESULTS SHOULD YOU HOLD THE EXPERIENCE ACCOUNTABLE FOR?

Your journey through *ENGAGED!* is almost over but your journey to becoming a more trusted leader who manages a branded experience is just beginning. Before sharing with you my concluding thoughts (I will keep them short as I know what it feels like to be at the final pages of an intense read and I realize how excited you are to turn the ideas shared into actionable results) let's have one more visit with the concept of measurement. The second part of the book (Principles 5, 6, and 7) provided tools and techniques for measuring,

Case In Point

Who?

A regional bank

What's the challenge?

- Defined core values and basic behaviors, but struggled to get workforce thinking about and delivering the experience consistently
- Semi-annual behavior consistency assessment scores were middle of the road and flat over time
- Difficulty communicating about the core values and making them relevant to the workforce

What did they do?

- Refined the core values and established a more clearly defined set of simple and actionable behaviors
- Continued ongoing evaluation of behavior consistency through semi-annual surveys
- Continued ongoing strategic recognition program efforts around the core values
- Instituted an approach that required each manager to add the company values to his/her regularly scheduled weekly meeting as sixty seconds spent highlighting an example of the experience in action

What was the result?

- 10% increase in behavior consistency scores within six months of using the sixty-seconds approach
- 700% increase in strategic recognition within six months of using the sixty-seconds approach—huge increase in stories of the experience in action, i.e., employees delivering the values to each other and customers
- Management more ENGAGED than ever, finally realizing that Living the Brand is a management strategy
- Within one year, ranked as the #7 best company to work for in New York

communicating about, and creating a culture of responsibility for living the branded experience—that is, managing and measuring the experience.

- Principle 5 explored the Know It and Do It Scores and the Employee ENGAGED Index as metrics for understanding alignment, engagement, and behavior consistency, as well as the ENGAGED status for any specific area of your company—metrics that provide actionable business intelligence.
- Principle 6 introduced the Customer Loyalty Index as a way to measure satisfaction and loyalty as part of a Customer Engagement Program.
- Principle 7 presented a strategic recognition approach to capturing and sharing successes, best practices, and Living the Brand Moments as a way to link employee behavior and experiences delivered to company objectives and financial results.

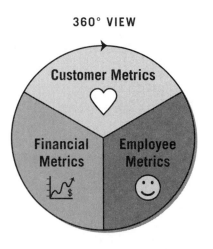

360° VIEW

These are three very specific ways to measure the branded experience and provide your company with a 360° View. Once again, ask yourself, what other business metrics are you going to hold the branded experience accountable for? (Reference the Metrics That Matter Most chart on the following page.)

Metrics That Matter Most

Which metrics should you hold the experience accountable for?

Revenue Generating
1. Repeat business per customer
2. Average sale per customer
3. Profit margin
4. Customer retention
5. Number of referrals
6. Average sale per top 20% of customers
7. Cross-selling/up-selling
8. Hours billed (utilization)
9. Inventory turns
10. Billing cycles
11. Conversion rates

Other: _____
_____
_____

Cost-Reducing
1. Employee turnover
2. Unwanted employee turnover
3. Quality issues
4. Product returns
5. Employee absenteeism
6. Legal expense
7. Marketing expense
8. Training expense
9. Safety issues
10. Time to fill a job
11. Employee theft

Other: _____
_____
_____

Consider any and all key metrics that drive your business that you currently track. I recommend picking at least two that you and your leadership team can track progress against.

As a manager in an enterprise it's an important part of your role to keep people focused on results. Managing the Experience provides you the perfect opportunity to look at your company from a 360° View. Look at the employee metrics that indicate cultural strengths and weaknesses. Look at the customer metrics indicative of loyalty and retention. And

Follow the link http://engagedbook.com/metrics to download a copy of the Metrics That Matter Most chart.

look at the financial metrics that most impact the profitability of your company. By looking at the experience from these different angles, keeping other people focused on these results, and using the tools and techniques provided throughout this book, you'll be more effectively Managing the Experience and building trust in you as a leader. At the very least you will be sparking those meaningful conversations that will create an environment of open communication where expectations are clearer and willingness to be accountable rises.

MANAGING THE EXPERIENCE IS NOT "ANOTHER THING"

I have one final insight to send you off with. This insight will be critical as you are sure to encounter the following situation and you must know how to respond. Some people may feel as though employees in their work area are already ENGAGED and delivering a consistently awesome customer experience. Or some may feel as though all this "branded experience" stuff is simply another thing they need to focus on. This will be particularly the case if your company has been guilty in the past of flavor-of-the-month-type activities—starting and stopping initiatives with a lack of "stick-to-it-iveness." In any case, it will be critical to get the following message across. You will need to say it over and over again at first. Yes, you will need to REMIND them of it!

Managing and delivering our company branded experience is not *another thing* to do. It's *the thing* we do.

Every day at work an experience is being delivered. The question remains: in the future, will you be managing it?

NO MORE TIME TO PAUSE. TIME TO TAKE ACTION!

Based on what you've learned, what are the first three things you can commit to doing to Manage the Experience?

1.

2.

3.

Citations

INTRODUCTION

1 (PAGE xx) A 2013 study found that 49 percent of executives believe customers will switch brands due to a poor customer experience. Even more interesting is that the same report found that 89 percent of customers say they have switched because of a poor customer experience.
  - Oracle, *Global Insights on Succeeding in the Customer Experience Era*, February 4, 2013.

2 (PAGE xx) The three drivers and how often they happen are:
  - Employee was rude: 73 percent
  - Employee was too slow to resolve my issue: 55 percent
  - Employee lacked the necessary knowledge: 51 percent
    □ RightNow Technologies, *Customer Experience Report, North America 2010*, October 2010.

PRINCIPLE 1

1 (PAGE 6) "All the world's a stage and all the men and women merely players."
  - Shakespeare, William. *As You Like It*. (Act II, Scene 7).

2 (PAGES 12–13) So then I share wisdom from Peter Drucker, Harvard Business professor and management guru, who published a paper

in 1986 stating that the purpose of every company is to create a customer.

- Drucker, Peter F., *Management: Tasks, Responsibilities, Practices* (New York: Truman Tally Books/E.P. Dutton, 1986).

3 (PAGE 13) According to research by Harris Interactive, consumers not only want a better experience but they will pay more for it. Even in a negative economy, 60 percent of consumers say a better experience is a high priority and one that they are willing to pay more for (either most of the time or always).

- RightNow Technologies, *2009 Customer Experience Impact Report*, October 2009.

4 (PAGE 13) On the flip side, another study found that 91 percent of unhappy customers will not willingly do business with your company again.

- Help Scout, *75 Customer Service Facts, Quotes & Statistics*, May 2012.

PRINCIPLE 2

1 (PAGE 15) The research tells us that 70 percent of workers are "not engaged" or are "actively disengaged" in their work, meaning they are emotionally disconnected from their workplace and are less likely to be productive. That leaves nearly one-third of workers who are "engaged," or involved in and enthusiastic about their work and contributing to their companies in a positive manner.

- Harter, Jim, "Monday's Not So 'Blue' for Engaged Employees," Gallup® Wellbeing, July 23, 2012, www.gallup.com.

2 (PAGE 16) A picture of CEO Danny Wegman accompanied the article with a quote that summed up the mindset that makes the company so successful, "The only way to be a great place to shop is to first be a great place to work."

- Dobbin, Sean, "Wegmans ranks No. 4 on list of best places to work," *Democrat and Chronicle*, January, 20, 2012.

3 (PAGE 19) Does it horrify you to know that it was recently reported that 65 percent of workers are either somewhat or totally unsatisfied?

- Adams, Susan, "New Survey: Majority of Employees Dissatisfied," *Forbes* online, May 18, 2012, www.forbes.com/sites/susanadams/2012/05/18/new-survey-majority-of-employees-dissatisfied/.

4 (PAGE 19) According to Gallup's latest findings, 70 percent of American workers are "not engaged" or "actively disengaged" in their work, meaning they are emotionally disconnected from their workplaces and are less likely to be productive. That leaves nearly one-third of American workers who are "engaged," or involved in and enthusiastic about their work and contributing to their organizations in a positive manner.

- Harter, Jim, "Monday's Not So 'Blue' for Engaged Employees," Gallup® Wellbeing, July 23, 2012, www.gallup.com/poll/155924/Mondays-Not-Blue-Engaged-Employees.aspx.

5 (PAGES 19–20) In the article, "Majority of American Workers Not Engaged in Their Jobs," Nikki Blacksmith and Jim Harter from Gallup share perspective on how over the past several decades (not years) researchers have identified a strong relationship between employees' workplace engagement and their respective company's overall performance.

- Blacksmith, Nikki and Jim Harter, "Majority of American Workers Not Engaged In Their Jobs," Gallup® Wellbeing, October 28, 2011, www.gallup.com.

6 (PAGE 20) A study from the research firm, the Economist Intelligence Unit, reported that 84 percent of top executives believe disengaged employees are one of the top three threats facing their business.

- Economist Intelligence Unit, *Re-engaging with engagement: Views from the boardroom on employee engagement,* The Economist Intelligence Unit Limited 2010.

7 (PAGE 20) Research tells us that Americans who have at least some college education are significantly less likely to be ENGAGED in their jobs than those with a high school diploma or less. Additionally, workers aged 30 to 64 are less likely to be ENGAGED at work than those who are younger or older.

- Blacksmith, Nikki and Jim Harter, "Majority of American Workers Not Engaged in Their Jobs," Gallup® Wellbeing, October 28, 2011, www.gallup.com.

8 (PAGE 21) In 1990, only 17 percent of jobs required knowledge workers. According to the McKinsey & Company report, *The War for Talent*, that figure has risen to 60 percent and continues to rise.

• Michaels, Ed, Helen Handfield-Jones, and Beth Axelrod, *The War for Talent* (Boston: Harvard Business School Press, 2001).

9 (PAGE 21) She told me about a study her firm conducted that revealed 80 percent of senior leaders believed their companies delivered superior customer service, while only 8 percent of their customers agreed.

• Allen, James, Frederick F. Reichheld, Barney Hamilton, and Rob Markey, "Closing the delivery gap," Bain & Company, 2005.

• Rogers, Paul and Jenny Davis-Peccoud, Bain & Company, "Leading from the Front" (Publication presented at the European Business Forum, December 1, 2005).

10 (PAGE 23) In fact, for three straight years, employee engagement has been the lowest in recorded history.

• Aon Hewitt, *Trends in Global Employee Engagement*, March 2011.

11 (PAGE 23) In fact, a recent study indicated that 63 percent of employees experience a high level of stress at work and 39 percent cite workload as the top cause of stress.

• "Presenteeism on the Rise as Employees Show Fatigue From a Slow- to No-Hire Economy," ComPsych press release, October 29, 2012, on ComPsych Web site, www.compsych.com/press-room/press-releases-2012/678-october-29-2012, accessed February 2013.

12 (PAGE 23) In the book, *The Enemy of Engagement*, authors/researchers Mark Royal and Tom Agnew report that nearly one-third of employees lack the resources and information needed to do their jobs. One-half are bothered by "inadequate staffing levels in their work areas."

• Baldoni, John, "Workplace 2011: Overworked and under-engaged," CBSNews.com, January 12, 2012, www.cbsnews.com/8301-505125_162-57326757/workplace-2011-overworked-and-under-engaged/.

13 (PAGE 24) Lack of Engagement Is Expensive

- 70% of ENGAGED employees indicate they have a good understanding of how to meet customer needs; only 17% of disengaged employees say the same.

  □ KPMG, "The real value of engaged employees," 2011.

- 78% of ENGAGED employees would recommend their company's products or services, compared to 13% of disengaged employees.

  □ Flade, Peter, "Great Britain's Workforce Lacks Inspiration," *Gallup Business Journal*, December 11, 2003, http://business-journal.gallup.com/content/9847/great-britains-workforce-lacks-inspiration.aspx.

- 75% of leaders have no engagement plan or strategy even though 90% say engagement impacts business success.

  □ Accor Services, *Reward to engage*, whitepaper, 2008.

- 84% of employees were searching for a new job in 2012. That compares to 60% in 2010.

  □ "Survey Finds Wide Employee Discontent," Right Management press release, November 29, 2011, on Right Management Web site, www.right.com/news-and-events/press-releases/2011-press-releases/item22035.aspx, accessed February 2013.

- ENGAGED organizations grew profits as much as three times faster than their competitors. Highly ENGAGED organizations have the potential to reduce staff turnover by 87% and improve performance by 20%.

  □ "Corporate Leadership Council Identifies New Roadmap to Engagement," Business Wire press release, April 11, 2007, http://ir.executiveboard.com/phoenix.zhtml?c=113226&p=irol-newsArticle_print&ID=983769&highlight=, accessed February 2013.

- Increased employee engagement was accompanied by a 12% increase in customer satisfaction and significant double-digit revenue and margin growth over the past three years.

  □ CBI, *Transformation through employee engagement*, March 2011.

14 (PAGE 28) Pink notes that the "science is very surprising and a bit freaky. We as humans are not as predictable as you might think." He points out that if you reward employees for things you don't always get what you are looking for with respect to additional motivation. In fact, the research shows that if a job requires even rudimentary cognitive skill (which is just about every job in your company) that higher financial rewards lead to poorer performance. This is contrary to conventional wisdom that the higher the reward the higher the performance..

◻ Pink, Daniel, *Drive: The Surprising Truth About What Motivates Us*, RSA Animate; 10 min., 48 sec. video. http://vimeo.com/15488784.

15 (PAGES 28–29) Pink says, "Money is a motivator but in a strange way." You must pay people enough to take the issue of money off the table by paying a fair market wage. Once the fair wage is covered, more compensation will not improve their happiness or performance and, in fact, often demotivates.

Pink points out three primary motivators that drive happiness and engagement at work:

1. Autonomy: The desire to be self-directed. More ENGAGED workers are able to thrive in a self-directed environment.

2. Mastery: The ability to get better at what we do. People feel good when they are challenged and able to focus on improving themselves or something they are working on.

3. Purpose: The feeling that you are making a difference.

• Pink, Daniel, *Drive: The Surprising Truth About What Motivates Us*, RSA Animate; 10 min., 48 sec; video. http://vimeo.com/15488784.

16 (PAGE 29) Teresa Amabile and Steven Kramer (authors of *The Progress Principle*) present another fantastic pathway for understanding what creates happiness at work and leads to an ENGAGED workforce—quite simply, making progress at work. It has been proven as a top motivator, yet its power is widely misunderstood by leaders. Of all the activities and happenings that can impact a person's mood and motivation at work, the single most important is "*making*

progress in meaningful work." Although this may seem quite obvious, it is anything but to most managers.

- Amabile, Teresa, and Steven Kramer, "Do Happier People Work Harder?" *The New York Times*, September 3, 2011, www.nytimes.com/2011/09/04/opinion/sunday/do-happier-people-work-harder.html?_r=0.

17 (PAGES 29–30) To prove this point, the authors conducted a study that asked 669 managers from companies around the world to rank the importance of five factors that could influence motivations and emotions at work. Four of the items came from conventional management wisdom: recognition, incentives, interpersonal support, and clear goals. The fifth was "support for making progress in the work." The results of this study revealed total unawareness of the power of progress across all levels of management. Support for making progress was ranked dead last as a motivator and third out of five as an influence on emotion. The concept of "progress in my work" simply is not on the radar of enough managers. Amabile and Kramer noted that across all the companies they studied, only rarely could they identify managers who consistently supported their people in making progress.

- Amabile, Teresa, and Steven Kramer, "Do Happier People Work Harder?" *The New York Times*, September 3, 2011, www.nytimes.com/2011/09/04/opinion/sunday/do-happier-people-work-harder.html?_r=0.
- Amabile, Teresa, and Steven Kramer, "The Progress Principle: Optimizing Inner Work Life to Create Value," *Rotman Magazine*, January 01, 2012.
- Amabile, Teresa, and Steven Kramer, *The Progress Principle: Using Small Wins to Ignite Joy, Engagement, and Creativity at Work* (Boston: Harvard Business School Publishing, 2011).

PRINCIPLE 3

1 (PAGE 35) They understand that culture is quite simply "the way we do things around here."

- Kotter, John P., *Leading Change* (Boston: Harvard Business School Press, 1996).

2   (PAGE 43) "Saving people money so they can live better."

- Walmart, "Our Story," http://corporate.walmart.com/our-story/.

3   (PAGE 43) "Think differently and positively change lives."

- Isaacson, Walter, *Steve Jobs* (New York: Simon & Schuster, 2011).

4   (PAGES 47–48) John Kotter, a Harvard business professor and world-renowned expert on organizational change management, makes the following point, "The central issue is never strategy, structure, culture or systems . . . The core of the matter is always about changing the behavior of people."

- Kotter, John P., *The Heart of Change* (Boston: Harvard Business School Press, 2002).

5   (PAGE 48) The late Stephen Covey, author of *The 8th Habit*, wrote about one of the most insightful challenges in our business world today. In his book he stated, "One of the greatest challenges that business leaders encounter is that of working to cascade and TRANSLATE the corporate vision from 30,000 feet into actionable line-of-sight behaviors among front-line workers to achieve critical objectives."

- Covey, Stephen R., *The 8th Habit: From Effectiveness to Greatness* (New York: Free Press, 2004).

PRINCIPLE 4

1   (PAGE 63) Remember from Principle 2: 80 percent of leaders tend to think their company delivers superior service while only 8 percent of customers feel they receive it.

- Allen, James, Frederick F. Reichheld, Barney Hamilton, and Rob Markey, "Closing the Delivery Gap," Bain & Company, 2005.
- Rogers, Paul, and Jenny Davis-Peccoud, Bain & Company, "Leading from the Front" (Publication presented at the European Business Forum, December 1, 2005).

PRINCIPLE 5

1   (PAGE 88) In today's work environment where 65 percent of employees are either somewhat or totally unsatisfied, you better believe they are willing to speak up and share why or why not.

- Adams, Susan, "New Survey: Majority of Employees Dissatisfied," *Forbes* online, May 18, 2012, www.forbes.com/sites/susanadams/2012/05/18/new-survey-majority-of-employees-dissatisfied/.

2 (PAGE 99) In the summer of 2006, I read an interesting book by Fred Reichheld (*The Ultimate Question*) about the single most important question for measuring how loyal customers are to your company. It's a basic recommend question: "Would you recommend our company to family, friends, or colleagues?" In his book, Reichheld shares ample research that suggests this question can provide a very accurate measure of customer loyalty. Respondents rate their likelihood to recommend on a zero-to-ten scale. The aggregate responses are then classified into one of three categories.

- Reichheld, Fred, *The Ultimate Question: Driving Good Profits and True Growth* (Boston: Harvard Business School Publishing Corporation, 2006).

PRINCIPLE 6

1 (PAGE 115) According to research by callcentres.net, 95 percent of companies collect feedback from their customers, yet only 10 percent actively follow up to do something about it.

- Bassett, Laura, "8 Best Practices for Customer Experience Management Today," *Avaya 2013 Guide: The Collaboration Trends*, (2013): page 114.

2 (PAGE 115) Another study reported that only 5 percent report back to customers that they acted on the feedback provided, and 69 percent of companies don't share customer feedback with their customer-facing people.

- 5%: "Using Customer Surveys to Improve Business Processes," Strategic Planning Research Note SPA-19-1128, E. Kolsy and M. Moaz, Gartner Group, February 7, 2003.
- 69%: "Operationalizing Customer Intelligence in the Contact Center," published in *Business Communications Review*, December 2007

3 (PAGE 115) In 2012, the Temkin Group reported that only 33 percent of companies use customer experience metrics to inform business decisions.

- Temkin Group, *The State of CX Metrics*, December 2012, www.temkingroup.com/research-reports/the-state-of-cx-metrics-2012/.

4 (PAGE 115) In fact, a study from the Customer Management Exchange Network reported that 61 percent of leaders cite customer experience management as their greatest challenge.

- Customer Experience Exchange Network, "CEM tops the poll as the greatest challenge for customer management professionals," US Customer Experience Exchange, 25th–26th September, Miami, FL, July 2012. www.customerexperienceexchangena.com/uploadedFiles/EventRedesign/UK/2012/September/21210001/Assets/Vendor-report-CEE-US.pdf.

5 (PAGE 117) According to a recent study reported in *Loyalty Management*, response rates from traditional forms of feedback (surveys, comment cards, inbound emails, Web site comments, and call-ins) is on the decline, falling from 50 percent in 2007 to 28 percent in 2011.

- Gambhir, Ashish, "The Next Generation of Customer Feedback Is Social Customer Satisfaction Intelligence," Loyalty Management, December 19, 2011, http://loyalty360.org/loyalty-management/2011-q4/the-next-generation-of-customer-feedback-is-social-customer-satisfaction-in.

6 (PAGE 118) The same study reported that as traditional feedback volume decreased, per store per year mentions on social feedback channels grew exponentially, skyrocketing from 450 to 9,330.

- Gambhir, Ashish, "The Next Generation of Customer Feedback Is Social Customer Satisfaction Intelligence," Loyalty Management, December 19, 2011, http://loyalty360.org/loyalty-management/2011-q4/the-next-generation-of-customer-feedback-is-social-customer-satisfaction-in.

7 (PAGE 118) A 2011 Global CMO Strategy survey stated that 70 percent of marketers say they feel incapable of analyzing and responding to the glut of data available about their consumers.

- "From Stretched to Strengthened: Insights from the Global Chief Marketing Officer Study," IBM Executive Summary, October 2011.

8 (PAGE 119) Two studies conducted with firms in the telecommunication and financial services industries show that only about 10 percent of Promoters (the respondents most likely to recommend the company to others) actually do bring in profitable new customers.

  - Lee, Bill, "The Hidden Wealth Beyond Net Promoter," *Harvard Business Review* Blog Network, May 10, 2012, http://blogs.hbr.org/cs/2012/05/the_hidden_wealth_beyond_net_p.html?awid=7338627826831586861-3271.
  - Kumar, V., J. Andrew Petersen, and Robert P. Leone, "How Valuable is Word of Mouth?" *Harvard Business Review*, October 2007, http://hbr.org/2007/10/how-valuable-is-word-of-mouth/ar/1.

9 (PAGE 123) Remember, 69 percent of companies do not share customer feedback with the individuals who are actually delivering the customer experience!

  - "Operationalizing Customer Intelligence in the Contact Center," published in *Business Communications Review*, December 2007.

10 (PAGE 124) For example, Apple has reported that for every hour their employees spend following up with "not satisfied" customers, they generate $1,000 in additional sales within six months.

  - Reichheld, Fred, and Rob Markey, *The Ultimate Question 2.0: How Net Promoter Companies Thrive in a Customer-Driven World* (Boston: Fred Reichheld and Bain & Company, Inc., 2011).

11 (PAGE 126) I recently read an article in *Harvard Business Review* about the importance of connecting employees to the end user. The article states that doing so drives motivation, productivity, and satisfaction because of three mechanisms: impact (employees see how they have an effect on the customer), appreciation (employees feel valued by the end user), and empathy (employees feel more connected and committed to helping another human being). One example shared found that introducing the end user to a group of call center employees led to increases of more than 400 percent in average weekly revenue!

- Grant, Adam M., "How customers can rally your troops," *Harvard Business Review* (June 2011): 99.

PRINCIPLE 7

1 (PAGE 149) A study done by the Society of Human Resource Management and Globoforce reported:

- 54 percent of HR leaders do not think managers and supervisors at their company effectively acknowledge and appreciate employees
- 69 percent of HR leaders believe employees are not satisfied with the level of recognition they receive at work
- 32 percent of CEOs invest no time in (and may not even be aware of) their company's employee recognition programs
  - Society for Human Resource Management and Globoforce, "SHRM Survey Findings: Employee Recognition Programs, Summer 2011," June 23, 2011, www.shrm.org/Research/Survey Findings/Articles/Pages/EmployeeRecognitionProgramsSur veyFindings.aspx.

2 (PAGE 150) How else can you explain how nearly one-third of CEOs invest no time or are completely unaware of the existence of their company's recognition program?

- Society for Human Resource Management and Globoforce, "SHRM Survey Findings: Employee Recognition Programs, Summer 2011," June 23, 2011, www.shrm.org/Research/Survey Findings/Articles/Pages/EmployeeRecognitionProgramsSur veyFindings.aspx.

3 (PAGE 151) Yet, companies spend more than $46 billion per year on employee rewards programs, and most managers still rely on bonuses, plaques, motivational posters, and other shiny trophy-like "carrots" to drive employee, and ultimately company, performance.

- Bersin, Josh, and Stada Sherman Garr, "A New Generation of Employee Rewards and Recognition Solutions: *The Achievers Offering*," Bersin & Associates Research Bulletin, September 8, 2011, Volume 5, Issue 44.

- Incentive Marketing Association, "Welcome to the Incentive Marketing Association," www.incentivemarketing.org/index.cfm.

4 (PAGE 152) The *Journal of Compensation and Benefits* found that fewer than 40 percent of HR managers believe their rewards programs drive measurable impact on employee engagement. Their research also showed that rewards programs are not viewed as initiatives that build and transform culture.

- Bersin, Josh, and Stada Sherman Garr, "A New Generation of Employee Rewards and Recognition Solutions: *The Achievers Offering*," Bersin & Associates Research Bulletin, September 8, 2011, Volume 5, Issue 44.

5 (PAGE 159) Even today, only 37 percent of HR leaders say they tie employee recognition programs to corporate values and less than half (43 percent) recognize employees based on performance related to the company's financial goals.

- Society for Human Resource Management and Globoforce, "SHRM Survey Findings: Employee Recognition Programs, Summer 2011," June 23, 2011, www.shrm.org/Research/Survey Findings/Articles/Pages/EmployeeRecognitionProgramsSur veyFindings.aspx.

6 (PAGE 159) Today more than 50 percent of U.S. mobile phone users are on a smartphone, and the percentage is increasing rapidly.

- "comScore Reports February 2013 U.S. Smartphone Subscriber Market Share," comScore press release, April 4, 2013, on comScore Web site, www.comscore.com/Insights/Press_Releases/2013/4/com Score_Reports_February_2013_U.S._Smartphone_Subscriber_ Market_Share, accessed May 2013.

7 (PAGE 167) Our informal research is further supported by an SHRM report stating that 44 percent of HR leaders don't feel that employees are rewarded according to job performance.

- Society for Human Resource Management and Globoforce, "SHRM Survey Findings: Employee Recognition Programs, Summer 2011," June 23, 2011, www.shrm.org/Research/Survey Findings/Articles/Pages/EmployeeRecognitionProgramsSur veyFindings.aspx.

8 (PAGE 168) Eighty-seven percent of companies do not currently track recognition program ROI, and 68 percent of HR leaders say they find it difficult to measure the effectiveness of their recognition efforts.

- Society for Human Resource Management and Globoforce, "SHRM Survey Findings: Employee Recognition Programs, Summer 2011," June 23, 2011, www.shrm.org/Research/Survey Findings/Articles/Pages/EmployeeRecognitionProgramsSur veyFindings.aspx.

PRINCIPLE 8

1 (PAGE 175) According to John Whitney, author and professor at Columbia Business School, "Mistrust doubles the cost of doing business."

- Whitney, John O., *The Trust Factor: Liberating Profits & Restoring Corporate Vitality* (New York: McGraw-Hill, Inc., 1994).

2 (PAGE 179) Studies show that only 10 percent of training is actually implemented.

- Hunter, James C., *The World's Most Powerful Leadership Principle: How to Become a Servant Leader* (New York: Crown Business, 2004).

Index

Index

T

Temkin Group, 115
360° View, xviii, 84–85
  Customer Engagement
    Program, 140–41
  Living the Brand
    Moments, 186–87
  Strategic Recognition
    Program, Living the
    Brand, 146
touchpoint, defined, 64
Touchpoint Wheel, 64–65
Tracy, Brian, 40
Transactional Experience
    program, 127–28, 133–34
trust building, leaders and
  branded experience as
    conversation, 181–84
  engagement, economics
    of, 174–76
  experience accountability
    and, 184–88
  highlights of, 173
  Manage the Experience,
    178–80, 188
  others opinions of, 176–78
Twitter, 118, 146, 165

U

Ultimate Question, The
  (Reichheld), 99, 119

V

very ENGAGED level,
    27, 109
visibility metrics, Living
    the Brand Assessment,
    93–94
voice of the customer
    (VOC), 117

W

Walmart mindset, 43
War for Talent, The
    (report), 21
Wegman, Colleen, 16–17
Wegman, Danny, 16
Wegmans, 16
Whitney, John, 175
What Else? Who Else?,
    119–121
work cultures and customer
    experience
  best places to work lists
    and, 35–38
  company intentions of,
    33–35
  defined behaviors and,
    46–50
  highlights of, 33
  mindset and, 39–43
  rating, xix
  visibility of, 38–39